THE FIFTY-MINUTE ESSAY

AND OTHER
TIMED WRITING

THE FIFTY-MINUTE ESSAY

AND OTHER
TIMED WRITING

Rebecca Roxburgh Butler
Dalton State College

HARCOURT COLLEGE PUBLISHERS

Fort Worth   Philadelphia   San Diego   New York   Orlando   Austin   San Antonio
Toronto   Montreal   London   Sydney   Tokyo

Publisher	**Earl McPeek**
Acquisitions Editor	**Julie McBurney**
Market Strategist	**John Meyers**
Project Manager	**Andrea Archer**

ISBN: 0-15-506965-9
Library of Congress Catalog Card Number: 00-105559

Address for Domestic Orders
Harcourt College Publishers, 6277 Sea Harbor Drive, Orlando, FL 32887-6777
800-782-4479

Address for International Orders
International Customer Service
Harcourt College Publishers, 6277 Sea Harbor Drive, Orlando, FL 32887-6777
407-345-3800
(fax) 407-345-4060
(e-mail) hbintl@harcourtbrace.com

Address for Editorial Correspondence
Harcourt College Publishers, 301 Commerce Street, Suite 3700,
Fort Worth, TX 76102

Web Site Address
http://www.harcourtcollege.com

Printed in the United States of America

0 1 2 3 4 5 6 7 8 9   170 9 8 7 6 5 4 3 2 1

Harcourt College Publishers

TABLE OF CONTENTS

PREFACE

Teachers who are accustomed to any of the traditional approaches to composition will find all the familiar terms and strategies right here. They are simply connected to a time line and a step-by-step explanation that students find particularly clear.

Like many authors of textbooks, I suppose, I began this one when I found the books available simply did not reach my students. I needed more on the writing process, something I could use in conjunction with our handbook. I focused on tying each step in planning, writing, and proofreading to a timetable. I also supplied more writing samples, samples as much like those written by college students as possible.

As I looked at my students' work and thought about what they needed to accomplish in a single term and what I needed to teach them, I pinpointed three broad areas for attention. No reader of an essay can help but notice these three elements: content, organization, and standard written English. Therefore, I shaped my lectures and class activities so as to achieve a balance of all three. I explained what I meant by content, how to stay on topic, how to recognize the differences between generalizations and specifics, and how to choose concrete language. I explained the usual rhetorical methods for structuring a written discussion, and also the basic beginning-middle-ending-with-transitions. I provided written guidelines and classroom practice for legibility, grammar, punctuation, diction, and sentence structure, emphasizing as most serious those errors that disrupt the main clause. And at the same time I focused repeatedly on timing, showing students how to create an awareness of the time they use in writing, how to estimate their word-per-line, word-per-page, and word-per-minute rates. We practiced allotting a reasonable amount of time for planning, drafting, and proofreading an assignment. Together we worked toward a balance of meaningful, specific content in an appropriate organization with few if any errors in standard written English, composed and proofread within a single class meeting.

As I actually wrote the pages of each chapter, I was aware of the student. Like all of us, students fear having their writing scrutinized and found wanting. Most of them, unlike more practiced writers, are not aware of the shifting states of mind they experience as they compose. And very few of them know how crucial writing will be to their career progress. Therefore, I have taken special pains to write in an encouraging tone and to show my student readers how to identify their strengths. I draw their attention to their *Creative Writer* and their *Editor.* They need to know that their abilities in thinking will not develop unless they write. They need to know that the best jobs require writing. So I have found opportunities to connect the material in this text with *real world* assignments and their marketability. True motivation comes from within, and once students discover that composition is not just an academic requirement to be lived through but a highly prized skill and theirs for the practice, they find the motivation.

DISTINCTIVE FEATURES

- The *Balanced Use of Time* chart serves as a one-page checklist with a time limit for each step in the planning, writing, and proofreading of an assignment with a deadline.

- *Brevity* makes the material more appealing to students to read in the first place and keeps their attention focused on the essentials.

- *Writing Samples* provide specific models on a variety of topics of the kinds of writing they may be expected to do.

- *Business Writing* models are included in the writing samples to suggest the value of writing beyond College.

- *Creative Writer* and *Editor* are the terms given to the states of mind needed for composing and proofreading, respectively. If a student is in the *Editor* mode when he should be composing, he will not get much written; if he is in the *Creative Writer* mode when he should be proofreading, he will not see obvious errors.

- *Answers to Exercises* allow students to pace themselves through the drill sentences and to improve their grasp of grammar and punctuation on their own.

CHAPTER ORGANIZATION

Chapter One, *Motivation, or, Why Write?* suggests some of the social and personal demands for writing as well as some of the rewards. In particular, it addresses ways for students to encourage themselves to succeed as competent writers. There is a section, too, on career marketability.

Chapter Two, *First Things First,* addresses the practical requirements of writing materials, legibility, and timing. It provides three writing samples and a list of typical topics. Most important for continued practice are the *Balanced Use of Time* checklist and a *Five-Paragraph Essay* schematic. A short section on the importance of reading concludes this important introduction to basics.

Chapter Three, *Planning,* explains, step by step, what to do in those first five to ten minutes, including tips on choosing a topic, consulting the dictionary, making notes and constructing a thesis statement. There are sections on vocabulary and on outlining and two writing samples.

Chapter Four, *Writing,* introduces the notions of *Creative Writer* and *Editor,* two very different states of mind necessary to effective writing.

Here, as well, are the traditional rhetorical patterns and argument, very briefly explained with examples. One of the writing samples comes from academia, the other from the world of business.

Chapter Five, *Proofreading*, explains how damaging a failure to proofread can be and which are the most important errors to remove. Each error is accompanied by ample examples, each example with its own notation. There are two writing samples, one a company newsletter.

Chapter Six, *A Final Word*, lists five brief rules for effective communication in nontechnical language: clarity, coherence, continuity, completeness, and courtesy. Specific rules of diction, grammar, punctuation, or paragraph development follow each rule.

Chapter Seven, *Exercises*, provides sixteen exercises for the most important errors in standard written English with an answer key. There is also a list of additional essay topics.

ACKNOWLEDGMENTS

I first want to thank my students, without whose efforts over the past thirty years this book would never have been written. The Dalton State College Foundation deserves special thanks for providing me with an entire term in which to work uninterruptedly on my manuscript. Some of my colleagues went the extra mile and not only read an early draft but gave me helpful suggestions, in particular, Frank Beesley and Wes Davis. For help with the Nursing material, I thank Trudy Swilling; for insights in Art, Beth Biron and for an introduction to Banking communications, Paula Klein.

I certainly want to thank my reviewers, Scott Douglass of Chattanooga State Technical Community College, Avon Crismore of Indiana University-Purdue University Fort Wayne, Bob Whipple of Creighton University, and Brooke Hessler of Texas Christian University. Their reactions were invaluable in helping me revise the original manuscript.

And sincere thanks to the Harcourt team, especially Gail Parker, Julie McBurney, and Jessie Swigger for their attentive listening and perceptive advice.

CHAPTER 1

MOTIVATION OR WHY WRITE?

There are a great many reasons for writing, some of which are discussed here. Sometimes we write because someone else wants us to write. That is called an external reason; it comes from outside ourselves. But ultimately the writer's motivation comes from within. So we begin in this section by exploring what you want and how to harness your own energies for writing.

PERSONAL SATISFACTION

Three of the strongest internal calls to write are for self-expression, for pleasure, and for self-improvement.

SELF-EXPRESSION

Perhaps you have heard the expression, "I don't know what I think until I see what I have said." This amusing line suggests how human beings depend on objectifying their experience in order to understand it. It is very much like looking at your reflection in a mirror to see whether you need a shave, a different color jacket, a hat. Inside our minds, our thoughts are in constant flux; our impressions may be strongly felt but vaguely defined. Writing them out clarifies ourselves to ourselves. Once we know what we ourselves think, we can make ourselves understood to others.

Then there is responsibility within the community. In a democracy, it is vital that individuals practice self-expression. Unless leaders hear what their people need and want, they cannot be expected to respond. There are always groups with the means of lobbying, getting the legislators' attention, for their interests. Senior citizens have a lobby in Washington, D.C.; large industries have their lobbies; environmentalists have a lobby, and so on. Individuals, too, deserve attention from their local, state, and national governments, and they can get it by writing to the men and women who represent them.

PLEASURE

Watch the face of a five- or six-year-old writing his name. That is genuine pleasure you see there. In part, it is the pleasure of mastery; controlling that marker or crayon, remembering the letters, and keeping the spacing even. There is also pleasure in naming one's self-identifying Me. She experiences another pleasure when she takes that writing, this name that means Her, and shows it to someone else—her mother, teacher, or grandfather. This is the beginning of communication, of sharing our innermost reality with others, a pleasure that meets one of the deepest human needs.

SELF-IMPROVEMENT OR HOW TO BRING OUT THE BEST IN YOURSELF

Here are a few ways to get and keep yourself in a productive frame of mind: Use encouraging words, find a study hideaway, look for like-minded friends, set goals, and give yourself rewards.

Never underestimate the power of encouraging words. Now this may sound strange if you haven't already discovered it for yourself, but think about the way you talk to an animal, a pet when you are praising it or trying to get it to do something new, something it doesn't understand or to teach it a command. Sweet little sounds are what we use with pets, babies, and other loved ones to convey friendly encouragement.

Now, some folks do seem to respond smartly to yells, grunts, and barked threats, and if you are one of these, by all means, take that commanding tone with yourself. In my experience, however, the severe style of instruction is too likely to provoke resistance, the last thing I want. It can even leave a scar behind. So when I need to change a habit or learn a new skill, I talk to myself (not necessarily out loud) as though I am my own child.

Seriously, earnestly, and tenderly, I tell myself how to do whatever it is, say, learn to write *I did* instead of *I done* or remember that *although* is a subordinating conjunction and not an introductory expression. I never call myself stupid and I never say, "I just can't do this." I fully understand that it may take some time for this change to sink in. I wouldn't expect to house-train a puppy in one day, and I do not expect immediate results with myself. I do not discourage easily. Every time I hear myself saying, *"I should of wrote,"* I stop and change it to *"I should have written."* I may have to repeat the correction five times, ten times, but I know that eventually it will stick.

Next, whether at your own home or the school library, a relatively quiet place with a desk or table, an upright chair, and a good light source is essential. You want this to be like your own little cave or treehouse, but uppermost, the place you get real work done. The first thing you may have to practice is just sitting still for an hour at a time. Have something specific to accomplish: homework, a number of pages to read, notes to recopy, or note cards to write for a research paper.

Like-minded friends can keep you happy with your choice to do what it takes to become a good writer. Do your best to get to know other students who are serious about studying.

Setting goals makes it clear what you want to accomplish and lets you measure your success. Just wanting to "be a good writer" is pretty vague. Goals can be small (all the better to count your successes), but they should be specific. Instead of telling yourself that you will memorize all the punctuation rules by Friday, pick something more manageable, such as the comma rules. In fact, a specific daily goal is an excellent motivator. Most of us find ourselves less likely to procrastinate when we have just one day to get it done.

Rewards! It is very important to reward yourself for work completed. If you do not recognize your successes, your motivation will evaporate. Now, these rewards do not have to be elaborate or expensive. For instance, sometimes there is nothing I want more than to sit in a comfy chair and stare out the window or watch ten minutes of television, a small bowl of popcorn within reach. I do not allow myself to do this *before* I complete my paperwork, only after, as a reward. If I have been working toward a big goal – finishing a long writing assignment or receiving an A in a course – then my reward will be greater, maybe a new sweater or tickets to a baseball game.

These are just a few of the ways to find that motivation you will need to persevere and finish the course you have selected for yourself. If you are interested in motivation as a subject or would like to see more examples, consult a psychology textbook or teacher.

CRITICAL THINKING

First of all, we need to understand that critical thinking is not negative thinking; "critical" in this phrase does not mean fault finding. Critical thinking looks for the important, the meaningful in a lecture, a newspaper article, or a textbook chapter. Critical thinking is analytical, meaning that it separates the parts of a whole in order to understand it better. A critical thinker can look at each sentence in a paragraph to see which one is the topic sentence, which ones supply the details and examples, whether or not there is a description or definition.

Writing makes us better thinkers and better readers because as we write, we go through the thought process of selecting the words and of creating the sentences to convey an idea. Having put together words, sentences, and paragraphs ourselves, we better appreciate someone else's paragraphs. Once I have written what I know about – for instance, my ideal job – I have discovered ideas I probably did not even know I had, and at the same time, I have become aware of gaps in my knowledge, things I would like to know. There are levels of thinking we simply cannot reach without writing.

HIGHER EDUCATION EXPECTATIONS

Very few entering freshmen realize that composition is not just one more course that they must get behind them, but one in which they either learn skills to take on into their next courses or they flounder. Whatever major the student chooses – business, computer programming, or criminal justice – those courses will require her to analyze and discuss ideas.

Harcourt, Inc.

First there are the textbooks themselves. In some you will see the kind of organization freshman English teaches: definition, comparison, classification, and cause-and-effect. In addition, there is a more sophisticated vocabulary, the technical terms at the heart of every discipline. Learning to understand the structure of paragraphs and essay discussion in composition class makes textbooks far easier to understand. Taking notes swiftly and efficiently, both in lectures and from texts, is a study skill recommended by all student counselors.

Second, in these college courses, the student will be presented with new ideas and asked to elaborate upon them, to define, to compare, and to examine causes-and-effects—in writing. These are the very basics of organization taught in freshman composition. Having mastered the building blocks of discussion in composition, the student will not put them behind him, but will use them to move more confidently into discussion questions and research projects, whether oral or written.

As you can imagine, unless a student gets herself into the habit of writing every day, she is likely to get bogged down in reading and writing assignments, if for no other reason than taking too long to capture ideas in notes and outlines. Writing efficiently is very important.

Because writing can mean the difference between passing and failing those more advanced content courses, many advisors recommend taking freshman composition as early as possible. You can motivate yourself to dive right in and become a writer by looking ahead and seeing what a difference it will make in your progress from freshman to sophomore to junior to senior year. And if you do not make the progress you expected to in that first freshman comp course, you do not give up or tell yourself that you cannot do it. You review what you learned during your first attempt, make a list of what you need to master, and go after it.

MONEY AND EMPLOYMENT

Very early pieces of writing, some surviving on clay tablets uncovered by archaeologists and translated by linguists, record business transactions. What could be more logical? Businesspeople, whether in ancient Mesopotamia or modern Atlanta, need to keep track of their inventories, negotiate contracts, and prepare and receive bills of lading and invoices. Accuracy and attention to detail are essential, and employees who can read and write to communicate competently and efficiently are valued.

As it was then, so it is now. Educators today are urged by businesspeople and by legislators to be rigorous in preparing students for earning a living. A new hire who cannot read piles of reports as well as write them is a disappointment; any job that will offer advancement will require writing. The minimum wage (no writing required) will be inadequate for anyone whose life will include paying rent and buying such essentials as groceries, clothing, and a car, not to mention paying for insurance and taxes. The best prepared graduates have the most options. Yes, it takes effort, and, human nature being what it is, making the effort is half the reward.

Harcourt, Inc.

At most colleges and universities around the country, big and small companies search for graduates at job fairs every year. Perhaps they should hang a banner on their booths: "GOOD WRITING IS THE ROYAL ROAD TO JOB PROMOTION." Accounting majors know how much accounting course work they need to be marketable, and pharmacy majors know how much chemistry they need, but almost no one seems to know that any job with good prospects for promotion involves lots and lots of writing. Here are just some of the kinds of written tasks most employees deal with every day or every week: many kinds of reports, purchase orders, memos, business letters, proposals, travel expense requests and reports, mission statements, assessment goals and results, and evaluation statements. The list goes on. Writing samples of some of these business documents are provided in later chapters.

Obviously, knowing how to write under pressure will make your workday easier. For the present, concentrate on learning how to manage your time while writing the very best English that you are capable of. And the best of luck to you!

Harcourt, Inc.

CHAPTER 2

FIRST THINGS FIRST

■━━━━━■

MATERIALS

This is a good place to talk about materials, the supplies that most writing teachers require and that you will want if you are teaching yourself. (Writing is one of those skills that all of us really teach ourselves.) The materials needed for producing presentable essays under deadline are few.

- A hardcover collegiate dictionary, most recent edition.
- Two ink pens (in case one stops writing), black or blue ink only (no erasable).*
- Fifty to 100 sheets of theme paper (regular or wide lined).
- A notebook or filler paper for making notes, planning, and drilling.
- A watch or clock [a built-in timer is useful (about $15 at a discount department store, such as Wal-Mart)].

Another valuable book to have is a good *thesaurus*, a very helpful tool in building vocabulary and learning to make good distinctions between words. If there is no college bookstore in your community, the collegiate edition dictionary can be ordered from any bookstore and the other supplies are available in most drugstores.

In addition to these materials, you will need a clean, flat surface on which to write, one in a place where you can concentrate. The area does not have to be completely silent, but you do not want to be interrupted. Your writing time and place must be protected.

---

* Pencil is out of the question. What most students like about the pencil is that they can erase any mistakes. But it takes too much time to erase. Remember, this is a timed activity. Putting a single, and only a single, line through a letter, word, or phrase is much quicker and neater. Secondly, pencil smears and rubs off on hands and clothing, something your readers will not appreciate. Pencil marks fade over time, too, so if you look back at notes you made early in a course, or perhaps in a former course, they may be barely legible. Finally, most directions for timed essays require ink, so you want to accustom yourself to writing in ink.

Harcourt, Inc.

TIMING AND LEGIBILITY

Now that you have your materials, you must learn how to put words on the page legibly and efficiently. This means, first, writing words of standard shape and size, leaving plenty of white space, and, finally, writing steadily enough to produce about ten words a minute. Not so hard, really.

First, then, *standard letter shape*: Take a look in penmanship practice books for grade-schoolers; these you can usually find in a drug-store. The cursive or handwritten letters that they present are good models. Basically, handwritten letters must be what readers expect to see, and not written so they are easily confused with other letters. For example, incompletely formed a's, o's, and u's can look alike; v's may look like u's; e's can look like i's, if i's are not dotted; circles instead of dots over i's make the whole word hard to read. Capital letters also must be a standard (easily recognizable) shape and larger than lowercase letters. The reader must be able to tell at a glance when a new sentence is beginning. For the same reason, words that should not be capitalized should not begin with large letters, and printed capitals must not be mixed in with cursive.

Next, it is the *white space* around letters and words that makes them legible. When letters are crowded together so that they touch or overlap or when words are strungtogetherlikethis with inadequate space between them, the reader's job becomes too frustrating.

Finally, each writer needs to know his own *words-per-minute* or *words-per-page* rate. Type-written pages total, on average, 250 words. But in a handwritten assignment, the total will depend on the size of your handwriting, and if you know how many words you are getting to a page, you will not waste time counting them as you write.

Take out a sheet of theme paper and a ballpoint pen and choose a simple topic such as "Describe what you saw on the way to school" or "Who is your favorite author and why?" Now, look at your wristwatch, note the time on your paper, and write steadily for five minutes.

You will do two counts. First, count the total words, omitting articles (a, an, the), and divide the word total by five. This figure is your words-per-minute. Now count the words on each line, for ten lines. Put the figure for each line in the margin, and then add the numbers for all ten lines. If your handwriting is smaller than average, you could get 7 on the first line, 8 on the next, 7, 9, 8, 6, 7, 9, 8, and 9 on the subsequent 8 lines for a subtotal of 78. The subtotal divided by ten = 7.8 or about eight words-per-line. Now count the lines on your theme paper. Say, there are twenty-three lines. You may need the top line for a title; you will definitely want to leave the bottom line blank for a bottom margin, so let's use the number twenty because it's a round number. Eight words-per-line times twenty lines, $8 \times 20 = 160$ words-per-page. Now you know that to produce a 400-word essay you will need to write three pages. Someone with larger handwriting may need to aim for four or even five pages.

Harcourt, Inc.

This is a good place to mention printing. Students often ask if it is okay to print, since their printing is more legible than their cursive handwriting. The problem with printing is speed, or, more accurately, the lack of speed. When we print, we lift our pen from the page one, two, three, or even four times *per letter*; when we write cursive, the pen stays on the paper from the beginning of the word to the end. Obviously, this method saves time. If you feel that your cursive penmanship is hard to read, practice writing to a rhythm. That is, listen for or feel the rhythm your hand creates as it lays down the slopes and curves of the letters of each word. Staying in a rhythm will help you keep to a standard shape.

To summarize the key points made in the preceding text:

- Get a wristwatch.
- Use standard, recognizable letter shape.
- Make capitals clearly larger; lower case letters clearly smaller.
- Leave plenty of white space between words.
- Figure out your words-per-line so you will know your words-per-page.
- Practice a rhythmic cursive so you will not waste time printing.

Harcourt, Inc.

WRITING SAMPLE

As soon as possible, a writing instructor wants her students to write something as a sample. This is usually something quite short, giving the teacher a chance to see the students' present skill level and giving the students a chance to determine what the teacher expects from them.

WRITING SAMPLE 1: AN IMPROMPTU ESSAY

Topic

Here's a writing sample on the writer's idea of the ideal teacher. Twenty minutes were allowed for writing.

My Ideal Teacher

Teachers are human, just like students, so none of them are completely
ideal. However, if I could have an ideal teacher, I would make him intelligent,
friendly, and fair.

Some students might want an easy teacher, but I prefer a teacher who really knows his subject and wants to teach it. What's the point of a teacher who
frag doesn't or can't help me learn? Someone who will come up with interesting
ways of getting the math formula or history lesson across to the class. An ideal
teacher should also be friendly, easy to talk to. Mr. Franklin, my high school biol-
ogy teacher, was very smart and very friendly. He always said some little some-
agr thing to every student as they walked into his room each day. He made time to
answer any question and never made a student feel stupid. Of course, the best
sp teachers are fair. Not only are they fair in gading and assigning homework, but
they keep the class in order. Teachers who let some students disturb the rest of
the class are not being fair to all.

I will be happy if my college professors have some of these qualities that
make teachers ideal.

Good content and organization!

There are few errors in standard English, but one is serious, the fragment beginning on line 6. Pronoun agreement also needs attention.

Correct each marked mistake in green or pencil, and ask me about anything you don't understand.

WHY AN ESSAY?

The timed essay test discussed in this book is a traditional measure of college students' abilities to express themselves clearly and correctly in an organized format. In many public and private American colleges and universities, students are asked to demonstrate that they are ready for junior (third year) level work by passing a basic writing or reading-and-writing test. Thus, the test has sometimes been called the Rising Junior Exam.

In Georgia, this pair of tests is called the Regents' Testing Program (RTP) and is offered on all state campuses every semester. One hour is allowed for the Reading Test, which is composed of several reading passages and questions about main ideas, details, vocabulary, inferences, and so on. Likewise, one hour is allowed for the Essay Test. The student chooses one of four general knowledge topics, that is, topics taken from personal experience and current events. After a few minutes of planning, he then writes a short essay that shows his ability to organize and develop a meaningful discussion in standard English.

The timed essay remains a favored testing instrument, not only by educators but by employers as well, because it reveals a good deal about a writer's ability to think critically as well as the level of his vocabulary and grammar. It reflects logic as well as imagination. It allows an individual to present his knowledge in his own way, in his own words.

There follow some examples of better-than-average timed essays.

Harcourt, Inc.

WRITING SAMPLE 2: AN IMPROMPTU ESSAY

Topic

It is now possible to shop for all sorts of goods on cable television. Given the choice, would you prefer to shop by way of television? Why or why not?

Television Shopping

Is it possible that our children will not know what department stores or shopping malls are? Television shopping can be a busy shopper's dream come true. Or so it seems. Actually, there are some drawbacks to this new shopping method. The viewer cannot search for a particular item, nor can she easily return an unsatisfactory item once purchased. Even worse is the possibility of becoming a television shopping addict. I have made a few purchases on QVC and decided that television shopping is not for me.

Most people like to comparison shop, and most of us like to see a wide choice of items before we choose. On the shopping channels, the viewer cannot search for that winter coat or a microwave oven, for instance. He can only choose from what is featured on any given day. When my Mom and sister decide it is time for new clothes, they begin by touring the local malls. Then they make trips to the nearby cities, making notes as they go. They also look through catalogs they collect. If they are in the market for a denim skirt or a party dress, they soon know every style, color, and price available. They can see and try on the clothing. Television shopping is too limited in this respect.

Another difficulty of purchasing over television is the time it takes to receive an order. Instead of driving home with my purchase and putting it to immediate use, I may wait several days or even weeks for it to arrive in the mail. And who is paying for the postage and handling? I am, of course. I once ordered a garden pruner after a friend bragged on one he had bought on television. After a week, I gave up, went to Home Depot, and bought a pruner I knew would do the job. When the pruner from the shopping channel did arrive, I could return it to the post office without any additional expense because I had not opened it. But if I had opened and used the item and then decided it would not do, I would have to wrap it back up and return it at my expense. Some of the items, unfortunately, look better on the small screen than they do in reality. And although everything seems to be on sale when it is shown, with an original price crossed out and a lower price displayed on the screen, once the viewer has that set of ovenware, or whatever it may be, at home and discovers it to be flimsy, the $49 plus $12 postage and handling may

---

not seem like such a saving over the list price of $60. Not only will he have to pay another $12 to return it, but he still has to shop for another set.

It was when I found myself sitting up late, night after night, just to see what sort of VCR, camcorder, or inflatable mattress might appear that I decided to change my ways. I overheard my friend Ron telling someone at a party that he had become "addicted" to QVC, and it started me thinking that I might be letting myself be hypnotized by those television salesmen. Ron was laughing about staying up "just a few more minutes" every night, only to discover that it was midnight when he finally went to bed. I had done that. He had run up his credit card one month without keeping track of the total. That had happened to me, too! It's the power of suggestion, he said. Aha, I thought to myself; this has got to stop.

I had believed that television shopping was a busy woman's dream come true, but how wrong I was! The choices were not good enough, the quality was hard to judge, and the payments were not really convenient. I decided that I had too many other worthwhile things to do than spend my life shopping on television.

WRITING SAMPLE 3: AN IMPROMPTU ESSAY

Topic

Should prison inmates be allowed to take college courses? Why or why not?

College for Prisoners?

It has been argued that it is unfair and inappropriate to provide college courses for convicted felons when deserving students must pay their own way. However, some prison programs encourage and even require some inmates to complete a GED or to take college course work in order to better prepare them for a law-abiding life after incarceration. Upon leaving prison, these former convicts will have spent their time constructively, be better prepared to earn a living, and thus be less likely to become career criminals.

How often have we heard complaints about the cost of housing and feeding prisoners, providing them with telephones and television? It seems that education is a pretty inexpensive option. Instead of learning from more experienced inmates more about burglary or money laundering, young offenders can be mastering algebra, improving their grammar, or reading American history. They could take computer repair or programming, depending on their abilities. Surely they will feel more confident after passing a college course, and more motivated to continue their education, than they would if they just sat in a cell day after day. Once a prison inmate has passed some college courses, he is more eligible for a decent job. An employer is interested in hiring someone who has shown the commitment to complete a course of study. It may not be easy to find employers who want ex-cons in their businesses, but someone with intelligence and persistence to succeed at the college level has an advantage. Furthermore, we should stop to realize that law-abiding students also receive State support in the form of education subsidies and scholarships. It is in society's best interests that its citizens are adequately educated and able to be self-supporting. If some got off to a bad start, all the more reason to train them. An inmate who has taken Math 101 has proven that he is trainable.

Perhaps the most important thing that education in prison can accomplish is to change the criminal's idea of himself. Instead of believing that he is meant to live as a thief or that there is no other way for him to earn money except to sell drugs, he may discover that he can change. Education by itself will not automatically make people better or change their circumstances, but it may be an experience the inmate likes. He may learn some ambition that will help him turn his back on crime as a career. Isn't it worth the cost of a college course?

Law-abiding, tax-paying citizens do not want prison inmates coming out of jail the same, or worse, than they went in. College credit courses can make imprisonment constructive and may help prisoners change for the better.

Harcourt, Inc.

TOPICS GROUPED BY SUBJECT

The following topics come from the University System of Georgia's Testing Program essay topics list. Here they are organized by subject. (Notice how many of these subjects match the sections in a newspaper.)

Family Life

- Should parents encourage their teenager to work part-time even if the family does not need the extra money? Why or why not?

- Do you eat breakfast? Why or why not?

- Is it better to be an only child or to have brothers and sisters? Explain.

- Some parents have begun to regulate the number of hours their children watch television by giving them a "television allowance" time. Do you believe this is a good idea? Why or why not?

- Is romantic love a sound basis for marriage? Why or why not?

- What are the most important skills and/or values children learn from their parents? Discuss.

Education

- Should every college student take a course in public speaking? Why or why not?

- Have you noticed any important differences between high school teachers and college professors? Discuss.

- Should high school students wear uniforms? Why or why not?

- Should college students postpone marriage? Why or why not?

- If you were asked to give some tips on studying to high school students, what would you advise? Be specific.

- How do you expect your college education to change the rest of your life? Be specific.

- In your opinion, what are some of the causes of violent behavior in schools? Go into some detail.

Entertainment

- Do you listen to radio talk shows? Why or why not?

- What is your favorite music and why? Be specific.

- Name your favorite game or sport and explain why you like it.

- Watching the "soaps" has become an American pastime. Why are these television shows so popular?

- Is there too much emphasis on spectator sports in our country? Agree or disagree.

The Workplace

- How does a job applicant go about making a good impression in a job interview?
- Name one job you would never accept and explain why.
- Should an employer have the right to test employees for drug use? Why or why not?
- If you could hold any job for one year, which job would you choose? Why?

Medicine

- Everyone who applies for a Georgia driver's license must choose whether to be an organ donor. Would you choose to be a donor? Why or why not?
- Do you favor or oppose the use of animal organs (such as hearts or kidneys) as transplants when human organs are not available? Why or why not?
- What do you do to cope with stress? Be specific.
- The "Living Will" directs a person's family and physicians not to keep that person alive by artificial means if that person were to suffer a totally incapacitating illness or accident. Would you consider signing such a document and giving it to your own family? Why or why not?

Personal Values

- If you were to win the lottery, would you save it or spend it? Explain.
- If you suddenly found your home on fire, and you could rescue only two or three possessions, what would you choose to save? Explain.
- "Manners belong to a bygone age; they are no longer relevant." Attack or defend this statement.
- How should students who cheat on their schoolwork be punished? Be specific.
- If you had the choice between a job you hated that paid $40,000 and a job you loved that paid $20,000, which job would you take? Explain.

BALANCED USE OF TIME

The time allowed for writing an essay could be as little as ten or fifteen minutes, or as much as six months, because the essay can be as brief as one page or as long as thirty pages, or more. It might be an impromptu assignment (one for which no preparation is allowed, sometimes called an in-class essay) or it might be one requiring library research. In other words, the essay is a very flexible form.

Still, the amount of time needed for the writing will correspond roughly to the essay's length. Most writers can produce fifteen words a minute without difficulty, and so they can produce 150 words in ten minutes or 450 words in thirty minutes. The important thing, however, is not to spend all your time writing. That's right. What is most important is to divide your available time into three parts, three unequal parts. No matter how little or how much time you are allowed as part of your writing assignment, you must allow about one-fifth of it for planning, about three-fifths of it for actual writing, and another one-fifth for proofreading. If you spend all the available time writing, the essay will be disorganized and riddled with mistakes.

One more thing, the frame of mind needed to plan and write is different from the frame of mind needed to proofread, to edit. I call the first mental state the Creative Writer and the second the Editor. They tend to get in each other's way if allowed to work together. In other words, do not let the Editor keep constantly interrupting the Creative Writer. With practice, you can learn to shift from one to the other consciously. It is essential to prevent the Creative Writer from using all the available time; he does not know how to proofread and does not care about it! The Editor needs about seven uninterrupted minutes to proofread sentence by sentence.

Here is a chart to guide you in making the most of your time, based on a fifty-minute assignment.

Planning (5 to 10 minutes)	1. If you have a choice of topics, go with the one that interests you most. Bring in your Creative Writer.
	2. Consider the topic phrase by phrase; check all key words in the dictionary and thesaurus.
	3. Free write, working in concrete nouns and action verbs.
	4. Formulate a thesis complete with subtopics and a closing
Writing (30 minutes)	5. Write steadily and legibly, shaping letters clearly. Do not crowd words or sentences.
	6. Use an organizational pattern that matches the question.
	7. There is no time for rewriting; make neat corrections if needed, rewriting clearly above the line.
Proofreading (5 to 10 minutes)	8. Take a minute's mental vacation; breathe deeply. Send out your Creative Writer; bring in your Editor.
	9. Read methodically, not for content but for glaring errors in grammar, punctuation, and weak development.
	10. Look with special care at the opening and closing; make your first and last impressions your best.

Harcourt, Inc.

THE FIVE-PARAGRAPH ESSAY FORMAT

This traditional short essay takes the typical form of five paragraphs, as diagrammed below. The first is a brief opening or introduction. Here the writer gets the main idea and basic direction of the essay stated. The next three paragraphs make up the "body"; now the discussion becomes specific, with supporting details and examples, one subtopic at a time. Then comes the closing, also short, which returns to the main idea and clinches it. Knowing this format and practicing it often will increase the speed of composition.

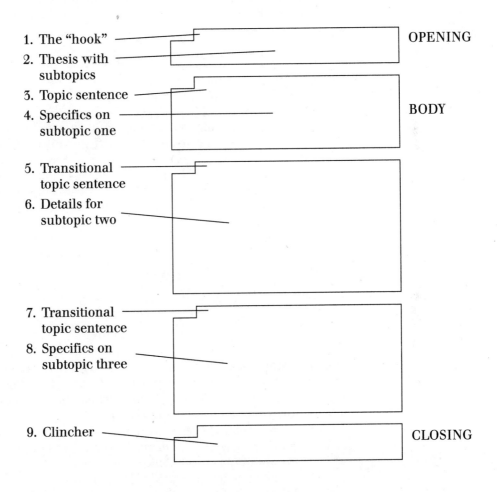

1. The "hook"
2. Thesis with subtopics

OPENING

3. Topic sentence
4. Specifics on subtopic one

BODY

5. Transitional topic sentence
6. Details for subtopic two

7. Transitional topic sentence
8. Specifics on subtopic three

9. Clincher

CLOSING

HAVING SOMETHING TO SAY, OR, HOW CAN YOU WRITE IF YOU DON'T READ?

Absolutely anything you like to read can make you a better writer: cookbooks, true detective magazines, sports columns, or gardening catalogs. I urge my freshman composition students to read something from the newspaper daily because news articles are similar to short essays and because current event topics frequently appear on the test list. Students can learn to have something to say on topics such as war, taxation, gun control, and the abortion debate by reading the newspaper.

Once I was teaching a General Equivalency Diploma (GED) course for several mill workers. The class was held on site, and they all came directly from working the first shift. After they cooled off, we would begin reading the lesson silently. One woman would inevitably break the silence with the words, "I just never liked to read!" She put all her frustration into that sentence. Several other women would encourage her, and they took turns helping her with her work, but she could not keep up. She talked of quitting. I thought and thought about what might motivate her. I asked her what she liked to do. All she ever talked about were her children and their sports. Her eldest son was then playing softball, so I suggested that she look for books about sports in the library, something the two of them could read together. She listened politely to my idea, but nothing more was ever said about it. Every day she would tell us about the game from the evening before. And every day, as she struggled to get through the textbook, she would wail, "I just never liked to read!"

Then one day it came to me what could change her mind. I waited until she came out with her usual refrain, "I just never liked to read!" and I said to her, "If you don't read, your kids won't read." And that was all it took. That was the reason she needed. She was quite a distance behind the others, who all completed their GEDs that spring, but she was determined. She caught up several reading levels over the year, and she received her GED the next spring.

So never underestimate the value of reading. Where do you want to be a year from now? You can keep on saying that you don't like to read, or you can get on with the reading you like.

READING

Students sometimes tell me that they are willing to read but cannot find the time. They are full-time employees or parents or both. They understand that reading is essential to their school success, but they genuinely do not know when they are going to do it.

Being a reluctant reader is as detrimental to your writing as having a small vocabulary. If you seldom read, you are unfamiliar with customary expressions and the usual sentence transitions and patterns. As you grope for a way to explain, let us say, why being an only child may limit a youngster's social growth, time is slipping away. Your mind may be quick, but if it lacks regular reading workouts, it is unequipped to put together your ideas clearly, promptly.

Those who seldom read are not even accustomed to seeing how sentences fit together in paragraphs. Naturally, their writing will be hesitant and laborious. For those of you who have not until now begun to read every day, here are some ideas.

First, find a book on something you are really interested in and carry it with you everywhere. Is there a sport you love, a hobby like gardening or cooking? Go to the library or bookstore (and look for the second-hand ones) and get an interesting book on your favorite subject. Now, keep it with you all day and take it to bed with you. With it nearby, you will be able to take advantage of those delays that happen every day to all of us. Stuck in traffic? Read a page of your book. Waiting at the doctor's office? Read your book. Here are some other opportunities for reading that you will want to be prepared for.

- Waiting for the roast to be done.
- Waiting for the dryer to stop.
- Waiting for the children to come out of school.
- Waiting in line at the discount store.
- Waiting to fall asleep.

You can think of others, I am sure. To use a metaphor, these are islands of time on which you can kick back and enjoy. If you always have a book with you, you will be surprised at how much reading you can get done every day. Just to prove to yourself how much reading you are getting done, keep a little spiral notebook and write down the time you start and stop reading.

Reading is feeding your brain. While you are devouring a romance and wondering if that handsome stranger is to be trusted, your brain is taking note of the different ways a sentence can be put together. It is collecting vocabulary and improving its spelling. Reading, like writing, makes it possible for you to think better.

WHAT READING TEXTBOOKS SAY

Reading textbooks often begin with paragraphs, showing the difference between the *main idea* and the *details*. These texts also emphasize vocabulary and teach numerous ways of understanding word meanings. Reading texts are famous for the formula SQ3R (Survey, Question, Read, Recite, Review). They explain the differences between *facts* and *inferences*. All in all, good reading texts guide the student in leaving behind his *passive* reading habits and show him how to become an *active* reader.

A SAMPLE TEST PASSAGE

[Sample test passages can be found in study guides for the GED as well as in reading textbooks.]

New Mexico is one of those states that seems to offer little to the Americans who look for economic vitality, good schools, well-developed social services metropolitan growth. One of the poorest states in the country as well as one of the driest, New Mexico's inhabitants depend on tourism, gambling casinos, military installations, and mining to bolster an economy with scant agricultural and industrial resources. What it lacks in material affluence, however, New Mexico more than makes up for in legendary figures. Two of its best-known characters are Geronimo and Billy the Kid.

Harcourt, Inc.

When he was born into an Apache band in the 1820s, Goyahkla, as Geronimo was then called, heard stories about the Spanish Army that was enslaving and killing Apaches as it sallied through the Rio Grande valley and along the Chihuahua Trail. When he was designated a warrior at the age of seventeen, Geronimo began what would be a life-long struggle against, first, the Spanish and, later, the United States government, which as early as 1855 was coercing Indians to sign treaties giving up their land.

Geronimo, not trusting the white man's word and hating reservation life, resisted for years. At last, promised cattle, horses, mules, farming tools, a house, and a large tract of land covered with timber, the great warrior signed. Instead, he was sent to Florida where he spent the next several years incarcerated or doing field labor. So famous had he become during the Indian Wars that in 1904 he was taken to the Louisiana Purchase Exposition in St. Louis where he signed autographs for twenty-five cents apiece.

Billy the Kid came to Santa Fe from Brooklyn, New York, in the early 1870s when he was still a youngster named Henry McCarty. There his mother married William Antrim, and young Henry McCarty became Henry Antrim. It was after his mother died of tuberculosis that the boy began spending time with William Shaffer, a petty thief. Sentenced to jail for a theft committed by Shaffer, Henry escaped by wriggling up a chimney and fleeing to Arizona. It was there he shot his first man at the age of fifteen.

Soon he returned to New Mexico with a new name, William Bonney. Partly because of his slim build and wavy hair and partly because he neither drank, smoke, nor consorted with prostitutes, he earned the nickname, "the Kid." Bonney was cheerful, charming, loyal, and generous, but he also possessed a hair-trigger temper and killed for revenge. He was convicted for his part as a member of the Regulators, a group who avenged the murder of their employer, John Tunstall. Under close guard while awaiting his hanging, Billy the Kid killed two lawmen and escaped. He was hiding in a friend's home when he was shot by Sheriff Pat Garrett in 1881.

Review Questions

1. New Mexico would be a good choice for a family with young children looking for a job and top-rated schools.
   a. True
   b. False

2. The word *scant* means
   a. scattered
   b. few
   c. multiple
   d. evenly spaced

3. The *general* or *main* idea of paragraph one is that
   a. New Mexico flourishes because of casino gambling.
   b. New Mexico's population as a whole is not affluent.
   c. In contrast to its relative poverty, New Mexico is rich in stories of larger-than-life frontiersmen.

    d. Geronimo and Billy the Kid are among New Mexico's founding fathers.

4. In the second paragraph, some *details* about the government's treaty with Geronimo include which of the following?
   a. Geronimo was considered a warrior at age seventeen.
   b. Geronimo did not trust the promises of the government soldiers.
   c. Cattle, horses, mules, farming tools, and forested land were promised.
   d. Geronimo was carried off to Florida and confined.

5. Based on Geronimo's imprisonment in Florida, the reader can *infer* that
   a. the chief was correct in his mistrust of the white man.
   b. the Indians had broken the treaty.
   c. the soldiers intended to kill the chief when they could.
   d. Geronimo died in jail.

6. William Bonney was born as
   a. William Antrim   **c.** Pat Garrett
   b. William Shaffer   **d.** Henry McCarty

7. The reader may *infer* that his mother's death had what influence on young Henry?
   a. led him to drink
   b. made him hate his stepfather
   c. left him in the company of Shaffer
   d. left him in the care of Pat Garrett

8. Which of these statements of fact convey the idea that Bonney was a complex and contradictory character?
   a. Billy the Kid killed two lawmen and escaped hanging.
   b. Partly because he neither drank, smoke, nor consorted with prostitutes, he earned the nickname the Kid.
   c. He shot his first man at the age of fifteen.
   d. Bonney was cheerful, charming, loyal, and generous, but he also possessed a hair-trigger temper and killed for revenge.

CHAPTER 3

PLANNING

■══════■

An essay that is not planned in writing will wander and repeat itself; in fact, it will read like planning notes instead of an organized essay. As the timing chart shows, there are four particular things to do quickly before you begin writing that first paragraph: Choose a topic, check the dictionary, free write, and formulate a thesis statement.

CHOOSING THE TOPIC

Sometimes there will be only one topic or question provided. In such cases, you do not have to choose, and this saves valuable time. Often there are three or four topics to choose from. And while most students feel more comfortable when given a choice, this can become a stumbling block if time is wasted looking at one topic after another, returning to the top of the list and considering them all again. The clock is ticking. It is imperative to be decisive.

How do you make up your mind? Well, you may get lucky and see that one of those topics is meant for you. It seems to leap out at you. Perhaps you just spent the summer on your first part-time job, and one of the topics is "What can a young person learn from working while going to school?" or "Is it beneficial or harmful for students to work part-time?" You know immediately that you have something specific to say. You have chosen your topic.

On the other hand, after reading all four topics, you may feel that you are drawing a blank. Here's how to break through that inertia and choose the topic that will work.

1. Draw a line through the worst topic, the one you do not even want to think about.

2. Look for one that interests you, even somewhat, or that you or someone in your family has some experience with. You are looking for a topic you know a little about, not necessarily something you love.

3. Avoid the mistaken belief that the topics determine how well you can write. Students can be heard complaining that they could not write because they did not get a "good" topic. (Looked at that way,

there are no good topics.) Remember, the topics have been selected precisely because they involve experiences everyone has had or has seen in the news. It is true that the topics usually sound really bland, boring even. This is because they are worded as generalizations; the wording is in the most general terms so that the hundreds of students taking the test can respond in any way that suits them best, with whatever they know. Keep in mind, then, that the topics will be general, but the essay must be specific. It is the writer's job to make the topic interesting.

MOVING FROM A GENERAL QUESTION TO A SPECIFIC ANSWER

GENERAL QUESTION	SPECIFIC ANSWER
1. Do high schools put too much emphasis on athletics?	Football players are treated like gods at my high school. They get a special lunch menu, they finish the class day early, and they are given tutors to keep their grades up.
2. What does music do for you?	It's amazing how bouncy music, like show tunes, makes me smile, makes me more energetic, and slow country ballads make me want to lie down and dream.

THE DICTIONARY

As soon as you've chosen the topic, open your dictionary and check all the key words. Even if you think you already know the words' meanings, there are some important benefits to consulting the dictionary.

1. You want to avoid misreading a topic and thereby writing off-topic. For example, a number of students have misunderstood the word *corporal* in this question: "Should parents use corporal punishment to discipline children? Why or why not?" Had these students realized that they should be discussing *physical* punishment, like spanking, as a means of training or teaching good behavior, they would not have written about withholding money or privileges when children break rules.

2. You want as full an understanding of the topic as possible as you begin planning. Reading the definitions for the key nouns, verbs, and adjectives will give you more ideas than you are likely to think of on your own, as well as synonyms.

3. You can check the spelling.

DICTIONARY EXERCISE 1

Check the dictionary for the **plural form** of the following words. The regular plural ending is -s, so it will not be listed.

1. box _____

2. child _____

3. city _____

4. freshman _____

5. hero _____

6. leaf _____

7. mouse _____

8. sky _____

9. tooth _____

10. wage _____

DICTIONARY EXERCISE 2

Note that there are typical endings (suffixes) for different parts of speech. Check the dictionary for the given words below and write in the related forms, usually located nearby.

VERB	NOUN	ADJECTIVE / ADVERB
1. create		
2.	decision	
3.		engaging
4.	harmony	
5.	hatred	
6. infuriate		
7.	immunity	
8.		indicative
9. laugh		
10.	negation	
11.		obedient
12. prefer		
13.		resolute
14.	terror	
15. weigh		

VOCABULARY

FINDING THE RIGHT WORDS

In keeping with our focus on time and the rate at which we write, the first thing to mention about vocabulary is this: The bigger your personal word treasury, the less often you will have to stop and search the dictionary. It may take two or three minutes each time you turn from your paper to the dictionary, even when you have a pretty good idea of how the word is spelled. You could lose ten or twenty minutes that way. Daily attention to noting down words new to you, and collecting and finding opportunities to use those new words will be extremely valuable: You will build a vocabulary that will be quite satisfying in itself and which will save you time.

But there is another very important reason for expanding your vocabulary. As someone who reads more than eighty student papers a week, I am convinced that when students have trouble finding something to say, the trouble is usually that they lack the words to say what they want. Let me give an example. Let's say the topic is this one: "Can learning a foreign

---

More and more people from other countries are coming to America to improve their lives. Some people say that if they want to come to this country, they should learn English, but it would be smart for us to be able to understand these people who could be employees and customers. It would be good for a person to learn a foreign language if he goes to another country, at work, and just to make friends.

I went to Mexico with my parents last year on vacation. Because I had taken Spanish in high school, I was able to ask directions to our hotel and to save my dad from ordering something weird at dinner. A person on vacation or on a business trip could feel very lost if he did not know the language of the country he was visiting. For instance, if a person left something at home, like a toothbrush, how would he ask for one if he did not know the language? And there are some things in every language that are just not said; a person could embarrass himself or his host by saying the wrong thing.

One does not have to go outside the country to hear a language he does not understand. At the grocery store, at the mall, and at work people from Hispanic and Asian countries are speaking their languages. Understanding the language of people we work with can make a big difference. When people around us are speaking a language we do not know, we may feel funny. But it is easy for people to learn a few words and phrases of their language and feel more at ease. This is what I have done where I work, and I can tell they like it.

---

language be beneficial?" The student has a vague sense that it is valuable when traveling to know the words for ordering from a menu or asking directions. He may live where the numbers of Asian or Hispanic immigrants are on the rise, so he realizes that he may need to communicate with them, possibly in their language, in school and the workplace.

With this much in mind, the student plans this thesis:

> Learning a foreign language can be beneficial for a person traveling to another country, at work, or just to make friends.

Notice that the subtopics are not parallel, a problem related to limited vocabulary. But we will leave that for the moment and simply read the first few paragraphs of the essay. It will be easy to see that a working vocabulary of only a few hundred words is a real stumbling block in thinking and writing.

Rather than analyze these paragraphs line by line, I will mention just a few words: *a lot, thing, big, good,* and *person* are vague and inexact. Notice that there is too much pointless repetition. Words like *bilingual* are expected for such a topic.

WHICH WORD?

Which word from the list below offers the best answer to each question?

1. Which puts off or postpones until later?
2. Which looks at or examines closely?
3. Which word fills with dismay?
4. Which threatens loss or injury?
5. Which overstates or enlarges to an abnormal degree?
6. Which word gains or comes into possession of something?
7. Which destroys or defeats through treachery?
8. Which reveals a secret?
9. Which passes beyond or rises above usual human limits?
10. Which one permeates, through and through?

---

acquire	jeopardize	sabotage
appall	obliterate	scrutinize
divulge	pervade	tolerate
exaggerate	procrastinate	transcend

Verbs

1. acquire   *to get, procure, obtain*

She hoped to acquire new friends, new skills, new possessions.

The goal of science is the acquisition of new knowledge.

An acquisitive person is focused on collecting things and money.

Harcourt, Inc.

2. **appall**   *to horrify, shock, overcome with fear*

Pictures of wrecked cars with bodies sprawled nearby appall most people.

Spitting in public shows an appalling lack of hygiene and manners.

Related words: *dismay* (arouse, alarm); *abash* (to make ashamed or embarrassed); *harrow* (terrify, torment); *petrify* (stiffen with fear – literally, turn to stone).

3. **divulge**   *to disclose or reveal*

Professional magicians do not divulge their secrets.

Divulgence of a client's confidence by a lawyer is unprofessional.

Related words: *Exposure* is often a scandalous disclosure. A *revelation* is a mystery or secret opened up or explained. Someone alert may *unmask* a fraud. The guilty may *confess* their crimes.

4. **exaggerate**   *to overstate, magnify, inflate*

Someone eager for recognition may exaggerate his abilities.

Calling the rain shower the Storm of the Century was a deliberate exaggeration.

This biography is a good, unexaggerated account of Babe Ruth's career.

Related words: *Adulation, idolization,* and even *eulogy* spring from exaggerated views of a person's worth. *Hyperbole* is poetic exaggeration. *Caricature* is the exaggeration of certain details of a face, a plan, or a work of art, usually for amusing or satiric effect.

Antonyms: *Underestimate, belittle, deflate, depreciate.*

5. **jeopardize**   *to endanger*

Unthinking physical punishment jeopardizes children's lives every day.

He puts his life in jeopardy by speeding and other kinds of careless driving.

6. **pervade**   *spread through, permeate*

Smells of disinfectant pervade every room and hallway of the hospital.

The Christmas spirit becomes pervasive in December.

Synonyms: *permeate, saturate, diffuse.*

7. **procrastinate**   *to delay, put off*

Almost everyone claims to procrastinate about seeing the dentist.

While usually viewed as a fault, procrastination can sometimes be a way of giving the mind needed time to work through a problem.

There is a club for procrastinators with the motto, "Never do today what you can put off until tomorrow."

The Latin word *cras* (tomorrow) appears in procrastinate and helps explain its meaning.

8. **sabotage**   *willful destruction of property, especially in strikes or war*

Competition can sabotage a friendship.

The Union soldiers sabotaged the Confederacy by tearing up railroad tracks.

Fear of sabotage led to the imprisonment of Asians in California during World War II.

9. scrutinize   *to examine closely*

Mother would scrutinize the vegetables for signs of decay.

By walking confidently with head held high, the thief hoped to escape the scrutiny of the police on patrol.

Compare to *inscrutable* which comes from the same Latin root, *scrutari*, to search carefully.

10. transcend   *to rise above or beyond, especially
the material or human*

The artist's goal was to transcend the traditional expectations for a realistic portrait.

The climax of the Beethoven symphony is a transcendent moment for the audience.

Notice the Latin prefix *trans-*, which means across or beyond and appears at the beginning of such words as *transport, transatlantic, transverse, translate,* and *transfer.*

Nouns

1. celebrity   *a widely known person*

A political celebrity like John Fitzgerald Kennedy is a bit different from a sports celebrity like Joe Dimaggio.

The Hollywood star system strove to create celebrities and thereby increase sales.

2. custody   *keeping, care, under guard*

The police may take someone into custody for his protection or for imprisonment.

The maintenance supervisor for a building may also be called its custodian.

3. dilemma   *a predicament, agonizing choice*

The soldier found himself on the horns of a dilemma; if he followed orders, he would be killing civilians, and if he did not follow orders, he would be court-martialed.

The dilemma is a common one: Find a way to cut expenses or go further into debt.

Related words: A *quandary* is a state of great anxiety or *perplexity*, which is not, like a dilemma, a matter of clear-cut alternatives. An *impasse* is a deadlock or dilemma with no acceptable solution or escape: The strike had reached an impasse; neither side would compromise.

4. eccentric   *odd, peculiar*

Bernard's obsession with taking rabbits everywhere he went led to his being considered an eccentric.

My aunt's eccentricity seems harmless enough: She wears only blue.

Related words: An *anomalous* occurrence such as snow in June is irregular, abnormal, and unexpected. An *aberration* is a defect in character or vision, which causes deviation from what is normal, right, or logical. *Capriciousness* is unpredictable behavior, subject to whim. *Idiosyncrasies* are minor peculiarities of personal behavior, like biting one's nails.

5. fidelity   *faithfulness*

It was Lt. Rider's fidelity to his vows as a policeman that won him the trust of his men and that of his neighbors.

The term high fidelity in an electronic sound system has to do with the accurate reproduction of the signal.

6. gratuity   *a favor or gift in return for service*

There is often a bit of controversy about whether those who earn low salaries should be given a gratuity – and how much.

The look on the waitress's face told everyone that the gratuity was too little.

Related words: While the word *gratuitous* is built on the same root, *gratu-* meaning pleasing or free, its meaning is quite different: A *gratuitous* comment is uncalled for, unprovoked, and unappreciated.

7. incentive   *stimulus, that which stirs one to do or be*

The bonus questions provide incentive for students to know more than the bare minimum.

Dad could not believe that the cars were both washed until he learned that Mom had promised $5 per car as an incentive.

Incentives usually come from someone or something in the environment, outside the person being influenced.

Motives are internal, within the person, although possibly as a result of outside influences.

8. labyrinth   *a maze, complicated network, or problem*

One of the earliest references to the labyrinth comes from the story of King Minos who had the master engineer Daedalus build a hiding place for the Minotaur.

The English love to build outdoor labyrinthian paths enclosed by high hedges through which visitors may wander at their leisure.

9. optimism   *tendency to expect the best*

His friend's optimism made the youngster decide to try harder to make the team.

Despite the experts' optimistic predictions, the stock market continued to decline.

Perhaps because she was an optimist, Vera seldom worried or had nightmares.

10. rancor   *bitter hatred, ill will*

The Wicked Witch of the West was filled with rancor against Dorothy.

Racism is a rancorous attitude toward anyone of another ethnic origin.

Related words: *Rancid* butter or other fat is spoiled or partly decomposed and thus bitter. *Rancid* and *rancor* come from the same Latin word, *rancere*, to have a sharp, bitter taste. *Rankle* comes from the Latin word *draco*, for dragon: Captain Ahab's loss rankled so deeply that it overcame his sanity.

PRACTICE SET 1

Find the word in from the lists that best replaces each italicized word or group of words in the sentences below. Use the plural or a different tense where needed.

1. Our group leader told us to *keep our eyes open* the bookcase for the map of the *tangled* underground escape route.
2. The witness was cautioned not to *give out* the arrangements that had been made for protective *care*.
3. The staff expected the *rich and famous* to be more generous with their *tips* than were the usual customers.
4. The investigators believe that the *dirty tricks* were motivated by *bad feelings* among the recently fired.
5. Her friends called her naive, but Susan knew that her *high hopes* sometimes let her *rise above* her failures and disappointments to succeed.
6. The hiring committee was *stunned* to learn that the applicant had *stretched the truth about* his glowing army record and awards.
7 Unless Henderson stops *putting off* on the plans for the recreation center, he is sure to *risk* the company's reputation.
8. The President's message was for us to find a way to make *commitment to* customer interests *carry through* every hour of our workday.
9. No one was really surprised when Bennett *got* that expensive collection of wigs because he has been an *odd-ball* for years.
10. The coach saw his *problem* as this: Give the team a *reward* and lose money, or not reward them and lose games.

ANTONYMS

Choose the word nearest to being exactly opposite in meaning to the italicized word.

1. *jeopardize*   **a.** to endanger   **b.** to lose   **c.** to keep   **d.** to protect
2. *celebrity*   **a.** professional   **b.** hermit   **c.** criminal   **d.** explorer
3. *fidelity*   **a.** brutality   **b.** uncertainty   **c.** inconsistency   **d.** treachery
4. *rancor*   **a.** devotion   **b.** anxiety   **c.** depression   **d.** relief
5. *sabotage*   **a.** to educate   **b.** to vacate   **c.** to defend   **d.** to defy
6. *exaggerate*   **a.** to transfer   **b.** to exhaust   **c.** to extend   **d.** to minimize
7. *appall*   **a.** to delight   **b.** to provoke   **c.** to question   **d.** to medicate
8. *divulge*   **a.** to cooperate   **b.** to contain   **c.** to confide   **d.** to hide
9. *optimism*   **a.** terror   **b.** belligerence   **c.** dismay   **d.** authority
10. *incentive*   **a.** impulse   **b.** obstacle   **c.** prize   **d.** coincidence

FREE WRITING

Once the topic is chosen and the key words are checked in the dictionary, the next step is to begin generating words on paper, looking for material to develop in the essay. The mind needs to be stimulated to supply the ideas it has stored away. Free writing lets the Creative Writer jot down more or less anything that comes to mind, keeping the hand and mind moving.

The idea is to write without stopping. Grammar and punctuation are unimportant here, and wandering off-topic is no problem; as soon as it can, the mind will get back on the topic. The only goal is to keep writing, because putting words on paper is a call to the brain to continue to supply words, and the longer the brain (or mind) is kept focused on this topic, the more ideas it will produce.

Putting your pen on paper is somewhat like putting your car key in the ignition and turning the key. If you sit at your desk with your pen in hand, thinking, your eyes gazing out the window, it's like getting in your car with your key in your hand and gazing through the windshield. In both cases, you are going nowhere.

The following example was written in four minutes on the topic "What would cause you to end a friendship?"

I can't think of many things that would make me end a friendship. You can't have too many friends. I have lost track of acquaintances, but anyone I consider a friend is a friend for life. Even Calvin, who became a Buddhist, is still a friend. I stay in touch with Connie and Shawn. You can't choose your family, they say, but you do choose your friends. Perhaps committing a crime?

What if a friend turned into a terrorist? Anyone who stole from me?

CLUSTERING

A slightly different kind of written planning is called *clustering*. Instead of a flow of sentences or phrases, clustering puts the free association of ideas around a central topic with connecting lines, so the "cluster" of topics and details suggests how the ideas can be related. Here is an example of the clustering method used on the same topic, ending a friendship. The time allowed for this writing was 4 minutes.

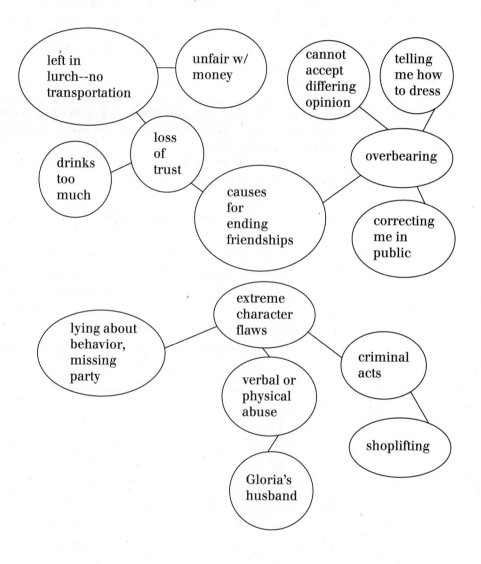

ACTION VERBS, CONCRETE NOUNS

If an essay is to be zesty, meaningful, and convincing, the important words must be exact, specific. The writer begins looking for these words during the planning stage. Using that topic on ending a friendship again, it is all too easy to lapse into wording like this:

> I want friends who are loyal and truthful. People who make fun of me behind my back or who are not there for me are not going to be my friends for long. I was good friends with a girl in ninth grade. We were together all the time for awhile. Then she started telling people things about me that weren't true. That was the end of our friendship.

What many teachers would probably write in the margin of this paragraph is the word *vague* or perhaps *general.* The wording is so general that the content cannot emerge. For instance, look at the verbs: want, are, make, are, are going, was, were, started telling, weren't, was. Almost all of the verbs belong to the category of *linking verbs* or *utility verbs.* The sentences need more *action verbs* for strength, life. Now look at the nouns: friends, people, back, friends, friends, girl, grade, time, people, things, end, friendship. Here are twelve nouns, and four of them, one-third of the total, are friends and friendship. The very general word *people* is repeated, and the vague word *thing* noticeably weakens that sentence.

It is not necessary to think about every noun and verb before writing the essay, but choosing a few and knowing what to avoid can make a significant improvement in the finished paper. For instance, the paragraph on "friends who are loyal and truthful" can be reworded slightly to put better emphasis on *nouns*: truth, loyalty. And what *verbs* would work here? How about friends who *break* trust or *betray* secrets? Maybe something about *losing* faith? Avoid the word *people* whenever it is possible to be more specific: classmates, so-called friends, colleagues at work, or fellow-workers. That second-to-last sentence can be improved all round by removing several wasted words and substituting the strong verb *lying*:

> Then she started lying about me.

Of course, some of these changes can be made during the proofreading stage, but unless the Creative Writer recognizes the need for this exact wording early, much time can be wasted and much fuzzy thinking will take the place of focused thinking as the essay is being composed.

Here's a short exercise to test recognition of action verbs and concrete nouns. Underline the more precise word or phrase. (Answers appear in the back of the book.)

Harcourt, Inc.

1 These groceries (are heavy; weigh thirty pounds at least)! 2 I (got a lot; bought enough for the weekend). 3 (There will be a lot of people; Twenty delegates have registered) for the retreat. 4 I (got a little bit of everything; decided on yogurt, bagels, bananas, and three kinds of juice) for breakfast. 5 If this meeting goes well, my boss (will be happy; can expect a raise).

CONSTRUCTING THE THESIS

The *thesis statement* is a sentence stating the *main idea* of the essay, the answer to the question posed in the topic. If the question was "If you won the lottery, would you save the money or spend it?", the thesis statement might respond "If I won the lottery, I would save half of it so that someday I can take early retirement, and I would spend the other half on a home and on travel."

Notice something about that example in the first paragraph; it does not say simply "I would save half and spend half." Part of the thesis statement's job is to preview the body of the essay, to prepare the reader for what is to come. This information matches the topics of the body paragraphs. (And it will be on the outline under roman numerals I, II, and III.) These preview terms are called *subtopics*.

Usually the subtopics come from the free-writing stage, the planning. There is a great deal in the free writing or clustering that can be discarded, but what is kept goes into the outline.

Here's another thesis statement, this one in answer to the question "Do you hunt? Why or why not?"

"It gives me great pleasure to hunt, probably because I began early, with my father and uncles, but also because I am so happy in the outdoors and because I am a pretty good shot."

One more: "What can be done to encourage citizens to report crimes they witness?"

"Few witnesses will report crimes unless they can feel sure that their reports will be taken seriously, that their work and family time will not be disrupted, and, most important, that they will be protected from retribution."

THE MEANINGFUL THESIS STATEMENT

A thesis is more than a statement of fact; it is a sentence that presents an interpretation, a preference, a position, an impression, an evaluation, a definition, a cause-and-effect, a proposal, a request, a belief, or any subject that may be seen from more than one point-of-view. In the examples below, some of the thesis statements are workable and some are inadequate. Explanations follow.

EXAMPLE 1

How is a college freshman like a first-grader?

1. A college freshman is very much like a first grader. [No thesis: This is not an answer to the question, but simply a restatement, without any conclusions, interpretation, cause-and-effect, or other explanation.]

2. A college freshman is going to meet many new people on his first day at school, just like a first-grader. [No thesis: A fact without any significance suggested.]

3. A college freshman may feel like a first-grader again, especially on the first day, wondering how he will find his classes, fearing that the teachers are ogres who eat students for lunch, and wishing desperately that he could just go back home. [Good thesis: The verbs, nouns, and adjectives all convey a state of mind, an interpretation, and there are subtopics for later development.]

EXAMPLE 2

Do you read the newspaper? Why or why not?

1. Reading the newspaper can be informative, entertaining, and educational. [Off-topic: The question calls for a first-person answer, such as "I read the newspaper because I find it informative, entertaining, and educational.]

2. Newspapers are largely taken for granted. Where would we be without them? I look forward to reading the paper almost every day. I prefer the local paper, especially the obituaries and the wedding announcements. And I can always find uses for the paper after I have finished reading it. [Rambling: Reads like free writing instead of a single sentence stating a clear central idea.]

OUTLINING

MAKING AN OUTLINE: FORMAL VERSUS ROUGH

For the purposes of an in-class, timed essay, a *rough outline* is sufficient. The thesis statement, the subtopics, an example or two will be all there is time for before writing begins. Without this sense of organization, remember, the writing will wander and become incoherent.

Again, using that topic on ending a friendship, here is a rough outline, including the thesis, the subtopics, and some supporting details.

THESIS: I seldom end a friendship, but when I have to, it will be because of a loss of trust, an overbearing personality, or some severe character flaw.

I. Trust broken—J. T. leaving me without rides, sponging money

II. The overbearing personality—Lois M. trying to force me to wear jewelry, her dress style

III. Extreme cases—some charming people are also drunks, abusive, thieves like Chuck D.

CLOSING: It's unusual for me to have a serious falling out with a friend, but some behavior is just not acceptable. When a "friend" abuses me, he isn't a friend.

A Note on Closings:

During planning students may feel unsure about how they will actually close the essay, and so they skip it, thinking that they'll decide when they get there. The strange thing is, they seldom do get there unless they already have an ending in mind. I mean, they just do not finish. It must be psychological. If you have a destination in mind, you are likely to reach it. So don't worry about the perfect wording, just jot down a closing that is consistent with the opening. You can improve it when you get there!

When there is a day or more to plan ahead, the *formal outline* may be required. This kind of plan follows a *notation system* and acts something like a skeleton for the essay. It includes the thesis, each subtopic and the supporting specifics in order, and the closing.

One of the Regents' topics asks "Is it better to have lived in one place all of one's life or to have moved around?" Here is a formal outline on that topic.

SAMPLE OUTLINE

THESIS: I look forward to pulling up stakes now and then because I loathe boredom, I enjoy seeing the country, and I overcome my fear of the unknown.

I. Despite security, boredom is poisonous

A. Too-familiar routines

B. Variety

1. New friends

2. Libraries, movies, Mardi Gras

(Continued)

II. A childhood move
  A. From cowboy country to Cajun bayous
  B. Food and language differences
  C. Friends for life
III. Conquering fear
  A. The first long train ride
  B. Worry replaced by excitement
  C. Adult love of travel
CLOSING: I am convinced that moving around has improved my life.

WRITING SAMPLE 4

This is the type of essay that might be assigned in a Composition I class. The topic is "Do you think it is better to grow up and live in one place all your life, or to move from place to place? Discuss."

Notice the mistakes in standard written English as well as the excellent specific content. (See Answer Key.) Assuming this to be a first draft, the writer can correct these errors legibly in the proofreading stage.

Give Me Variety and Change

Many of my friends have lived their entire lives in the bosom of their families in this town, and they love it. However, I wonder how they keep from being bored. I moved several times as a youngster, and to this day, I look forward to pulling up stakes now and then. I loathe boredom, I love seeing the country, and I have overcome my fear of the unknown.

While growing up in familiar surroundings, does provide a sense of security, too much sameness can be poison. If my family had not moved from a small town in Texas to a suburb of New Orleans. When I was eight years old, I would never have met Nancy Harris, who became my best friend. And I would not have had a library near enough to walk to, and I became an avid reader. In New Orleans there was Lake Pontchartrain; great seafood, and Mardi Gras. Then, when I was older, I moved to north Georgia and learned to love the mountains. I think variety has been important to my emotional health, and variety of scene has been exciting for me.

That childhood move from cowboy country to Cajun bayous open my eyes to nature. As the train crossed rivers heading south, the landscape changed from brown to green, trees grew taller, and brightly colored flowers

(Continued)

and birds appeared. Soon I was eating fried shrimp, crab cakes, and red beans and rice. I had been unhappy about leaving my School friends behind, but I loved my third-grade classmates Ruth, Norm, and Louis. And I stell have the fondest memories of Saturday movies at the Ogden Theater, just four blocks from our house. Today I have friends from California to Washington, D.C.

Perhaps the most beneficial effect of my moving here and there have been the confidence it has given me to anywhere. That first long train ride seemed scary when we climbed the high metal steps into the dark train, but the rhythm of the wheels on the track and the beauty of the countryside through the window overcame my fears. Likewise, in the next few years changing Schools and learning to ride the bus were scary at first. Deciding to pull up stakes again and go to the university or take a new job, these moves always began with a little anxiety but ended in excitement and a taste for adventure. To this day I love to travel, whether for pleasure or work, I have vacationed in New Mexico, Old Mexico, the Okeefenokee, Ireland, and Florence, Italy. I even worked for a year in eastern Europe.

There is no doubt that geographic mobility has improved my life, bringing me opportunities and adventures I would never have enjoyed otherwise.

Answer Key for Writing Sample 4

First line of ¶ 2, remove the comma after "surroundings."

Replace the period with a comma after "New Orleans" to avoid a fragment.

Replace the semi-colon after "Pontchartrain" with a comma.

Add an "ed" to "open" in the first line of ¶ 3.

Remove the capital S from the words "school" in ¶s 3 and 4.

Correct the spelling of "stell" to "still" in ¶ 3.

Correct the agreement error, line 1 of ¶ 4: change "have" to has.

In that same sentence, add the verb "go" after "to."

Toward the end of ¶ 4, change the comma after "work" to a period (comma splice).

WRITING SAMPLE 5

Here is an example of a type of in-class writing students may do in literature classes: the plot summary. Like taking class notes, the plot summary requires more active thinking than does just reading a piece of fiction or listening to a teacher discuss it. The aim is to identify characters and the conflicts they face, briefly but precisely, so as to show how one event leads to or causes the next.

Plot Summary of "The Child by Tiger"

The story is set twenty-five years in the past and narrated by Spangler, one of four young friends playing football in the neighborhood when the ball bounces loose. It is thrown back to them by the recently hired Negro handyman Dick Prosser. This black man, who works for one of their fathers, Mr. Shepperton, is described as "splendid" because he knows about football, boxing, shooting, and does everything to perfection. He keeps his room immaculate, reads his Bible and attends church. But there is something a bit ominous about his shadowy silence and red eyes.

One troubling incident occurs when the Shepperton car, chauffeured by Prosser, is run into by a car driven by the drunk Lon Everett. The offensive Everett strikes Prosser in the face and Prosser takes the attack without flinching, but his eyes turn red. The next odd thing is that Pansy Harris, the Shepperton's cook, gives notice without reason. There is no specific connection known between the two workers, but the uncertainty creates apprehension. Then, just before Christmas, two of the boys come into Prosser's room and find him with a rifle. Prosser urgently begs them not to tell their parents, explaining that it is a "supprise" for the "white fo'ks" and that he will teach them how to shoot it. And that night, the town's fire alarm rings to signal an emergency. Men followed by their boys dress hurriedly and rush to the town square: Prosser has killed six men. The crowd turns into a mob, refuses to proceed lawfully, forces open the hardware store, takes weapons and ammunition, and swarms out in pursuit with dogs.

Prosser had killed Pansy's husband and then methodically shot the policemen who tried to intervene. He then headed out of town. The manhunt continued all the next day, and it was the morning of the following day when they caught sight of him and closed in. After killing one more deputy with his last bullet, Dick did a curious thing. He removed his shoes, turned calmly, and faced the mob. The mob riddled his body with bullets, hung the lifeless body from a tree, brought it back to the undertaker's, and hung it in the window where the entire town, including the boys, came to see it. Sickened by the hatefulness they had been made aware of, the boys hear one of the crowd bragging about his part in Dick's death.

It was later that the survivors tried to put the story into perspective, and there were always rumors about Dick's past, but Spangler understood that the only answer they would ever have was the shadow left by the dark side of man's nature, which Dick had come to symbolize—both a "brother and a mortal enemy . . . a tiger and a child."

Harcourt, Inc.

WRITING

As you begin to write, become aware of the differing attitudes or outlooks that live in your mind when you compose, in particular, the Creative Writer and the Editor. When you are being inventive, trying out ideas, you are in your Creative Writer; when you are correcting spelling or punctuation, you are in your Editor.

THE CREATIVE WRITER AND THE EDITOR

The ideas, the words, and the sentences for the essay are all produced by the Creative Writer, that part of the mind that invents and arranges. The one thing that often stands in the way of the Creative Writer is the Editor. The Editor is that part of the mind that pays attention to form: grammar, legibility, and the like. The Editor can have a chilling effect on the Creative Writer if the two are allowed to work at the same time. Imagine someone trying to write with someone else looking over his shoulder saying, "Are you sure that's right? I think that's spelled wrong."

THE WRITER-IN-CHIEF

Now let's introduce a third viewpoint, that of the Writer-in-Chief–you. You must keep the Editor out of the room while the Creative Writer is composing. The Creative Writer's job is to produce 500 words in 35 or 40 minutes, but he will become hesitant and even inhibited, if the Editor interferes. Similarly, it is the Editor's job during the proofreading stage to check subject–verb agreement, correct fragments, and so on. But the Creative Writer loves his own words. He cannot see the errors. Keep him out of the room while the Editor is at work!

THE "HOOK"

The more standard term for "hook" is *audience appeal*. It is believed that audiences are motivated by basic needs: self-preservation, hunger, approval, and mastery, for example. The writer's aim is to lead the reader into the subject and to make him want to read on. Beginning the opening paragraph with the thesis statement is too abrupt, too bald. With a "hook" you create suspense, concern, horror, anger, surprise, shock, or humor. The "hook" can raise a question that needs answering. Here are some examples:

1. *Topic:* Ending a friendship

   "Hook": Would a friend borrow my car, wreck it, and tell the police I was driving? I think not.

2. *Topic:* Worst classroom distractions

   "Hook": During my history final last term, someone actually threw up, but most distractions are not that bad.

3. *Topic:* Why Americans own millions of pets

   "Hook": When irresponsible pet owners tire of their overgrown Christmas puppies, they just bring them to the pound. Here they are not "put to sleep," but killed by lethal injection.

4. *Topic:* Should public speaking be a required course?

   "Hook": My tongue was dry, my palms were damp, and my knees were locked: I was giving my first speech.

ORGANIZATIONAL PATTERNS

Look at these seven topics and ask yourself whether or not you would answer all of them the same way. That is, would you *arrange* your answers the same way? Would you outline your answer simply as "thesis statement, subtopic 1 with examples, subtopic 2 with examples, subtopic 3 with examples, closing"?

1. Describe your most prized possession. Explain why you cherish it.

2. Is it worse to have loved and lost, or never to have loved at all? Explain.

3. Name someone living today you consider a hero, and explain why you define him or her as heroic.

4. If you commute to school or work, you must be prepared for road problems. How do you keep yourself and your vehicle ready for road emergencies?

5. What are some of the causes of academic failure at the college level?

6. Who are the most dangerous kinds of drivers on our roads? Be specific.

7. "Winning is not the greatest thing, it's the only thing." Agree or disagree.

In order to match an answer to a question successfully, the writer needs to notice what sort of organization is implied, suggested by the question. Question 1, for instance, is a *description* question. It requires visual details, physical details, maybe sounds, or textures.

Question 2 calls for *comparison,* as the word worse indicates; and the question has two parts: to have lost love *or* never to have loved at all.

Question 3 asks for a discussion of the *meaning* of a word, hero. This makes it a *definition* topic, so the answer should supply definitions, meanings from the writer's viewpoint, using a particular individual as an example.

Question 4 asks *how*, which is the signal for *process* topics; the discussion will emphasize action, verbs, steps, and stages in a progression.

Question 5 asks for *causes*, which is the cue for a *cause-and-effect* answer. (Notice that effect is spelled with an *e*, meaning results.) Sometimes the question will ask for causes, for what produces a situation, and sometimes it will ask for effects, the consequences of some decision, habit, or action. Whichever the case, the writer will want to take both causes and effects into consideration in the essay.

Question 6 signals a *classification* discussion with the word *kinds*. To discuss kinds or types of something, we *divide* the topic according to some principle of organization. In this case, we are looking for drivers (the general topic) that are dangerous (the organizing principle).

Question 7 is a different "animal" altogether. It presents not so much another type of organization as a different purpose. The key words are "Agree or disagree." In other words, the writer is asked to take a position for or against. This instruction is the signal for what is known as *argument* or *persuasion*, and the sort of essay that defends or attacks is sometimes called a *position paper*.

DESCRIPTION

What does it look like? What does it sound like? What does it smell like? Is it warm, cold, heavy, damp, rough, bumpy, sweet, or itchy? Of all the ways of writing that bring an idea to life and engage the reader, none is more vivid than description. When my students write paragraphs that are too short or too general, the first thing I suggest to them is to add some description.

Read through this paragraph and see if it seems *vague* (inexact, uncertain, unclear, or general). The topic is "Describe your most prized possession."

My most prized possession is my dog. I feel very close to this dog because he was a birthday present from my uncle. He is a very loyal animal. For example, every day when I return home, no matter what time, he is waiting. He loves to play, and he loves to eat. He makes me laugh with his antics. I do not know what I would do without my dog.

This paragraph is well-organized and unified. However, the content is all generalized. Look at the wording. "Dog," "loyal," "play," and "antics" are all generic expressions, not specific, and there is no description! What breed is this dog? What color? Big or small? We need a word-picture of Buster bouncing around or slurping his Alpo.

See how much more engaging descriptive detail makes a piece of writing. Here is the same dog, but with a name, a color, a size, and one-of-a-kind behavior.

Lonnie, a 95-pound jet-black Labrador Retriever, is my most prized possession. He is more than a possession, really, more like a brother. Lonnie is named for my great-uncle Lonnie who passed away the year after presenting me with a silky, stumbling little creature, all legs and pink tongue. Even before he was a full year old, Lonnie took to "guarding" me at night, stretched out full length in my bedroom doorway. Very soon he figured out that the school bus dropped me off at 3:25. There he would be at the front gate, bouncing as high as he could. Now Lonnie can snag a high-flying Frisbee, and when he trots back, head up, he is the picture of self-satisfaction.

Here are some description topics.

1. If anthropologists unearthed your room in the year 3000, what would they learn from it about our civilization?
2. How much has your home/hometown changed in the past five years?
3. Where would you prefer to vacation, in the mountains or at the beach? Why?
4. Many college students now are commuters. What does it take to make a car road worthy for daily commuting in any weather?

COMPARISON

The comparison topic has a double subject, so during the planning it helps to keep two columns of notes, free writing, or clustering. The planning below is for Question 2, "Is it worse to have loved and lost, or never to have loved at all?"

LOSING LOVE

Losing love is painful, when a grandparent dies or the girl you have a desperate crush on ignores you. Imagine a spouse dying or divorce. Even losing a pet is wrenching.

NEVER LOVING

Never loving may not be suddenly painful, but it seems it would be empty. Imagine turning down pets because you couldn't bear losing them? Maybe it's the fear of losing a sweetheart that's as bad as the actual loss. Maybe not. Think of all you'd miss out on. Human beings are meant to be loving.

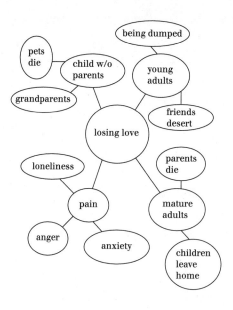

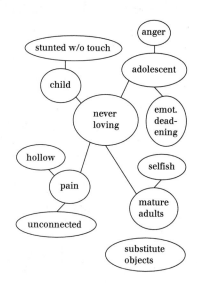

Outlining

Since comparison involves pairing, or a double subject, the body of the essay should reflect this duality. There are two arrangements that work well: *divided* or *alternating*. In other words, the discussion may first present all there is to say about loving and losing, then everything about never loving at all – the divided method. Or the body paragraphs may alternate from one subtopic to the other.

The two outlines below illustrate the two arrangements.

DIVIDED	ALTERNATING
Thesis: Losing love is better than never loving at all.	*Thesis:* Losing love is better than never loving at all.
I. Losing love teaches us what we value.	I. Children require love to flourish.
A. Childhood losses are overcome.	A. Neglected children are stunted.
B. Adolescent choice builds character.	B. Deaths of pets, grandparents are overcome.
C. Mature grief is a measure of love.	II. Young adults learn to love or perish.
II. The absence of love is deadening.	A. Suicide and murder: extreme but real consequences.
A. Babies who are not held fail to develop normally.	B. Rejection is painful, but some times love is returned.
B. Unloving adolescents are dangerous.	III. Mature adults cherish love despite its thorns.
C. Substituting food or possessions for love is unhealthy.	A. Inability to love makes life pointless.
Closing: Loss is inevitable, and love makes life worthwhile.	B. Grief is an expression of love.
	Closing: At every age, love makes life worthwhile.

DEFINITION

In an essay discussion, definition is more than the sort of brief phrase found in a dictionary. An essay definition is also called an *extended definition*. Definition essays are appropriate for ideas that are complex or personal, like the definition of the word heroic or the topic "The ideal teacher."

The usual way to extend a definition in organized paragraphs is by way of examples. The writer considers just what meaning or meanings to include and chooses as many striking examples as needed to be convincing.

For example, the writer may begin by mentioning some of the conventional meanings of heroism: physical courage, the willingness to sacrifice one's self for the good of the community or another, or someone who is exceptionally talented or larger-than-life. The writer may name some specific well known heroes, Patrick Henry, Florence Nightingale, Martin Luther King, Jr., and John Glenn. Then, the writer may wish to emphasize something unusual or more personal in her definition. Let's say that someone in the writer's family has been diagnosed with a life-threatening illness and has shown a spirit of optimism and determination that has heartened the entire family and could be considered heroic. Thus, the discussion becomes an extended definition of what heroism means.

Here are some definition topics:

1. "Human rights" is a term frequently used but seldom defined. What rights can be said to belong to every human being?

2. Do you consider yourself a conservative, a moderate, or a liberal? Explain.

3. What is your definition of a gentleman or a lady? Be specific.

4. Do you consider yourself a "goal-oriented" person? Explain with examples.

PROCESS

Many students find process organization one of the easiest to write. As long as the *steps* or *stages* of the process are mentioned and action verbs dominate, the discussion will succeed. The discussion singles out each part of a larger whole and shows the *sequence* of events. Here is a short example of a process.

In organizing an essay, it is good to follow the advice the old preacher gave the young beginner about sermons. "First, you tell 'em what you're gonna tell 'em. Then you tell 'em. And last, you tell 'em what you told 'em.

Notice the *transitional* words: first, then, last.

Here are some typical process topics. (Notice the signal word *how.*)

1. How can anyone make a good impression during a job interview?

2. What are some things a commuting student must do to make sure that his car is road worthy?

3. How does one make perfect pancakes / scrambled eggs / coffee?

4. How do you cope with stress?

CAUSE AND EFFECT

When an essay topic asks for an explanation of why something happened or what is likely to happen in certain circumstances, it is asking for a discussion of causes and effects. This method examines the *connections* between events, especially the *origin* or *reasons* for something or the *consequences* or *results*. Writers must be careful to be as logical as possible with cause and effect, to choose moderate language, watch out not to oversimplify, and to expect complex causes.

- Choose moderate wording and make reasonable distinctions.

cause 1

cause 2

more serious
causes 3, 4, 5

Example

In recent decades the reported death rate from cancer has been rising dramatically. How alarmed should we be by this statistical change? One cause of the increase is probably the simple fact that we are more aware of cancer than we were in the past, and that we are less ashamed of the fearful disease. Another cause may be that more people die in hospitals now and better records are kept. When folks died at home, the cause was usually listed as "old age." But factors like these take us only so far. Cancer seems to have been gaining ground in an absolute sense. If so, the real causes must be environmental: the increase in smoking, in the use of pesticides and food additives, and increased pollution from automobiles and industry. Some of those sources may be more responsible than others, but until we know more, we had better give serious attention to them all.

- Create meaningful transitions to keep causes and effects connected as you write.

  Incomplete. A group of Italian mothers has declared war against drugs and pushers.

  Corrected. As a result of their children's drug addiction, a group of Italian mothers *became desperate enough* to declare a war against drugs and pushers.

  Disconnected. Minority quotas in the job market should be discontinued. Quotas discriminate against the white male.

  Connected. Minority quotas in the job market should be discontinued *because* they discriminate against the white male.

- Be reasonable.

  1. The most frequent logical fallacy seen with cause-and-effect is hasty generalization, jumping to a conclusion without specific evidence.
  2. Few situations can be traced to a single, uncomplicated cause; do not oversimplify.

Here are some cause-and-effect topics:

1. What are the most frequent causes of failure at the college level? Be specific.

2. What can a student learn from a part-time job? Go into some detail.

3. Explain why you do or do not hunt.

4. Do you think that athletic competition is good for children under the age of twelve? Why or why not?

CLASSIFICATION

When a topic is made up of related *types, kinds,* or *subgroups,* classification is the organization needed. The outline, for example, is a classification system. Each Roman numeral marks a major division of the larger topic. Of course, the simple act of putting subtopics into an outline form does not create a true classification. Here's an outline that does not really make sense because there is no *organizing principle.*

Thesis: The best bargains are winter airfares, flea market furniture, and the classifieds.

   I. Winter air fares

  II. Flea market furniture

 III. Classified ads

Now, if we are going to discuss "best bargains," in order to be consistent, to have some stable basis for consideration, we must choose a single point that all our subtopics will share in common. The organizing principle, since the topic is bargains, could be price. The Roman numerals could be I. Bargains under $25; II. Bargains between $25 and $100; and III. Bargains over $100. Another way to organize kinds of bargains is by place. For instance:

Thesis: The best places to find the best bargains are in the classifieds, at garage sales, and on the internet.

   I. Classified bargains

     A. Autos, boats, bikes often half price
     B. Furniture (a couch for $25)

  II. Garage sales

     A. Baby clothes, toys, under $1!
     B. Dishes

 III. The internet

     A. Priceline.com (airfares for low bid)
     B. Auctions at ebay.com

Closing: Knowing where to look will save money.

Here are some classification topics:

1. Name the kinds of students you most like to have in class and explain why you so classify them.

2. Who are the most dangerous drivers on the road? Explain.

3. What sorts of television programs would you classify as unsuitable for children under the age of twelve and why?

4. What kinds of relaxation are especially beneficial to college students? Why?

ARGUMENT

Written argument is like a silent debate; if the reader is to be aware of the two sides, the writer must be knowledgeable about both pros and cons, even though she will favor one over the other. Another term for argument is *persuasion*; the writer may not so much disagree with anyone as try to gain something (like permission to use the car or a raise). This type of essay is sometimes called a *position paper*.

Argument goes beyond explaining a topic; it must be convincing. And there are five ways to make any argument a strong one. First use solid facts: names and numbers. Second, include graphic material; make the words paint a picture. Third, quote witnesses or experts who are in a position to know. Fourth, be reasonable; avoid exaggeration and impossible claims. Fifth, include the opposing view, not only to show your knowledge of the subject, but also to refute the opposition.

1. Always use factual detail instead of generalization.

vague

specific

> The numbers of visitors to national parks are increasing to a dangerous level. Too many people are clogging the roads, filling the air with automotive pollution, and littering.
>
> It would seem that Americans could never run short of wilderness areas to enjoy—there are 18,000 square miles in the ten largest national parks alone. But the truth is that the millions of annual tourists are threatening to overwhelm these sanctuaries. In the Great Smokies Mountains National Park, for instance, there are over nine million visitors each year, attracted in part by its 800 miles of trails and 170 miles of paved roads. Its lush forests shelter another attraction: bear, deer, and smaller animals. The Park Service is considering limiting the number of visitors per day, banning cars, and creating foundations to supply the money for maintenance that Congress has not funded.
>
> **The Atlanta Constitution, June 1, 1998**

2. Support your argument with graphic details.

vague

> When the plane went down it was snowing, but not heavily, and there was a light wind. Shortly after becoming airborne the plane veered to one side and turned over. There was screaming and then quiet. Rescue groups searched through wreckage scattered all along the runway. The last report was 27 dead.

word picture

> Snow was falling but visibility was 2000 feet and the crosswind only 11 mph when Continental Flight 1713 shuddered on takeoff, dipped to the right, and flipped off the runway into a small gully. Survivors report three explosions; then screams filled the cabin. As the fuselage skidded for three-quarters of a mile, mud and snow engulfed the passengers. "They were packed in there like fish in a cooler," one rescuer remembered. An airport spokesman described the debris as a "jungle gym of mangled metal." The DC-9 was in the air just six seconds, but it took rescue crews six hours to free the living and the dead from the wreck.
>
> **USA Today, Nov. 17, 1987**

3. Support the argument with witnesses and authorities. In the previous example of the plane crash, the information from survivors, the statement from a rescuer, and the description from the airport spokesman are all examples of support from witnesses. It is not always necessary to quote a witness or expert word-for-word; a paraphrase will do. For in-class essays, remarks or opinions from parents, teachers, local officials, etc., will do as authoritative or first-hand evidence.

4. Be reasonable. This is sometimes called having a *sound premise.* What this means is that if your main idea is illogical or untrue, the rest of the argument will be "bull feathers." For hundreds of years it was *believed* that the sun and all the planets and stars revolved around the earth; then, with the aid of the telescope, that premise was tested and disproved. Be careful not to use assumptions or beliefs as if they were statements of fact.

FACT OR SOUND IDEA	FALLACY OR QUESTIONABLE IDEA
Philadelphia is located 40° north of the equator.	Slaves were clearly happy because they sang.
Infants need stroking if they are to thrive.	Tom has a part-time job, so his grades will fall.
Venereal disease is spread by sexual contact.	Italians have large, loving families.

In March 1997, 39 members of the Heaven's Gate cult were found to have committed suicide in the group's compound, expecting to be taken to the next world in a spacecraft. The selection below comes from the Opening Message on their Web site.

unsound
premise

> Whether Hale-Bopp has a "companion" or not is irrelevant from our premise perspective. However, its arrival is joyously very significant to us at "Heaven's Gate." The *joy* is that our Older Member in the Evolutionary Level Above Human (the "Kingdom of Heaven") has made it clear to us that Hale-Bopp's approach is the "marker" we've been waiting for—the time for the arrival of the spacecraft from the Level Above Human to take us home to "Their World"—in the literal heavens. Our 22 years of classroom here on planet Earth is finally coming to conclusion—"graduation" from the Human Evolutionary Level. We are happily prepared to leave "this world" and go with Ti's crew.
>
> **www.heavensgatetoo.com/**

5. Strengthen the argument by refuting an opposing view. The natural tendency seems to be to ignore the opposition, but that may be interpreted as ignorance or fear. Instead, you can look both knowledgeable and smart by selecting a well-known opposition view and showing its shortcomings. Take, for example, the topic of the danger of guns in homes. The writer remembers a news article or a television story in which an Emory professor compared a large group of victims of gunfire inside homes with the same number of people in the same neighborhood (*The Atlanta Constitution*, Oct. 9, 1993). The study found that it wasn't strangers who caused the violence, but relatives and friends, and they weren't breaking in. Now, who would be the "opposition" in this case, someone who advocates gun ownership for protection? Yes, the National Rifle Association. So at some point in the essay, the writer wants to mention this organization's view and use the facts from this study to *refute* the idea that homeowners need guns as protection against intruders. Naturally, you are not likely to remember every detail from a news story while you are in class planning your essay, but whatever details you can recall will be sufficient. The reader does not expect you to provide complete documentation, just as clear a reference as you can.

Here are some argument topics:

1. "The best things in life are free." Agree or disagree.
2. Should animals be used in cosmetics research? Why or why not?

3. Should drivers repeatedly convicted of drunk driving have their cars confiscated? Why or why not?

4. In order to increase the opportunity for more registered voters to get to the polls, it has been suggested that we change our national voting day from Tuesday to Saturday. Agree or disagree with this idea.

WRITING SAMPLE 6

Fine Arts Essay Questions

In academic classes of all kinds, essay examination questions require the student to remember key terms, personalities, movements, innovations, dates, and so forth and to arrange them in paragraph form within the time allowed.

Here are some questions from a fine arts class that are intended to be answered in a full paragraph or more.

1. Explain the origins, the development, and the curriculum of the medieval universities.

2. Discuss the differences in Romanesque and Gothic architecture that correspond to differences in theological ideas.

3. Explain how a listener/viewer is invited to participate in the completion of an Impressionist work of art.

4. Describe at least three aspects of our own culture that have traceable roots in Greek culture. Give an example for each.

Here is a sample essay answer for question 4.

The continuing effects of Greek culture upon our own are numerous, including the political idea of democracy, the ideal of the Golden Mean, certain religious beliefs about death, dreams, and providence, and even the sport of wrestling. Three particular connections between the Greece of three thousand years ago and the America of today are the Greek alphabet, classical architecture, and the theater.

The Greek alphabet is the ancestor of all modern European alphabets. Developed about 1000 BCE, the Greek alphabet was notable for adapting former consonants into vowels, for example, alpha for *a*, epsilon for e, and iota for *i*. It was the Greeks who changed the direction of script. Before 500 BCE the lines ran right to left, but after a gradual change, all Greek script was written from left to right, just as English is to this day.

Perhaps the most visible influence Greek culture has had on our own culture is its architecture. Greek revival architecture became a dominant style in 19th century Europe because of widespread interest in recovered Greek works of all kinds. In America, Jefferson's Monticello and the columned

---

(Continued)

plantation houses of the deep South are both tributes to the golden age of Greek art.

Finally, theater as a Western art form began in Greece, and the Greek distinctions between tragedy and comedy are still very much alive in today's Broadway theater. Perhaps Neil Simon's comedy of manners can be considered a distant relation of the satires of Aristophanes. Arthur Miller's "Death of a Salesman" is clearly patterned after the tragedies of Sophocles in which the hubris of the protagonist brings disaster on himself and his family. The attention to structure and moral issues so dear to the Greeks seem destined to survive through our time and beyond.

The Greek genius for design, their appreciation of the individual quest, for intellectual attainment, above all for questioning and testing everything—these qualities have outlasted their time in the sun and have become standards to live by for the ages.

WRITING SAMPLE 7

Bank Memorandum

In a business setting such as a bank, memos convey necessary information from department to department, from management to entry-level employees, from co-worker to co-worker. It would not be unusual for a loan officer or a trainer to write several memos a day, each one composed in a matter of minutes or over the course of an hour or two, depending on the complexity of the information.

Here is a memo from the Training and Compliance Office of a bank where a long-term training program has been underway and is being assessed. The memo is addressed to the training officer's boss.

_____ **HB & T Training and Compliance**

Memo

To: Richard Wellford
From: Corrine Kenner
CC:
Date: 11/22/2000
Re: Thursday Planning Session

(Continued)

STRENGTHS:

Same as those noted in the revised plans of October 1999.

WEAKNESSES:

TRAINING

Training offerings during 1999 were attended by 60% of the bank's employees. Unless a session is "mandatory," employee attendance is often lacking because of "conflicts." This results in either an attitude that training is not important to the department / management or that the employees don't see this as a goal which will improve them as a team or individually.

Teller training is compromised by a lack of receipt printers and the lack of a "training bank" with accounts set up where actual deposits/withdrawals can be processed and receipts printed. Need to work closer with M&I and Christine to set up a training bank and need to purchase receipt printers for the 4th floor training room.

FACILITY

The chairs in the Highridge Room need replacing. Whenever a meeting exceeds two hours there are complaints that the chairs are "sat out" and have little or no padding. Many have loose or broken arms.

The lighting in the Highridge Room and the adjacent kitchen needs electrical work. Additional lights above the white board and on the podium will improve presentations.

The main office branch looks worn and in need of new carpet. We are projecting a look that says we are old and poor. The other banks Joy and I visited as "shoppers" looked much "healthier."

Goals:

1—Coordinate a "Job Exchange Day" where employees in different departments work two days per year in another department. This would provide some understanding of the role of the team and give growth to the individuals involved.

2—Establish an Employee Investment Group to work with a Trust Department employee who could supply financial acumen and assist in developing a small investment pool for limited amounts or even paper investments only.

3—Establish compliance training on the network—this is in progress. We need to insure management support of online time and commitment to complete required compliance training.

4—Review all job descriptions and policy/procedures. Some have not been updated/reviewed in a while. Network version needs cleanup/replacement with newest policies/procedures.

Chapter 5

PROOFREADING

■══════■

WHY STUDENTS DON'T PROOFREAD AND WHAT HAPPENS AS A RESULT

Had the essay on moving from place to place, "Give Me Variety and Change," Writing Sample 4, not been proofread, it would have failed. It contains too many serious errors: a fragment, an agreement error, and a comma splice. Students seem to find it difficult to stop writing as the end of the hour approaches. Their Creative Writer wants to write more and more. Caught up in the race against time, they throw away their only chance to clean up any errors that have occurred along the way. The Creative Writer has taken control and thinks that there is nothing more important than the wonderful words he is pouring onto the page.

The Writer-in-Chief must step in and see to it that this all-important proofreading gets done, banish the Creative Writer, and let the Editor get to work. One way to initiate this transition of power is to put your pen down. Sounds simple, doesn't it? You should see me try to get a classroom full of students to put their pens down when they are in the grip of their Creative Writers. It is simple, but only if a voice in your mind can interrupt that train of thoughts you are composing, only if you train yourself so that putting down that pen and clearing your head become automatic.

WHAT A PROOFREADER MUST KNOW

Ideally, every editor or proofreader is remarkably sharp eyed and notices everything from legibility to apostrophes, from verb tense to spelling, from cliches to commas. In practice, it takes years to develop that sort of eye. The freshman writer can aspire to that degree of thorough proofreading, but he absolutely must see and correct the really serious errors. These are mistakes in grammar involving the main clause. That means that the proofreader knows the basics of standard written English.

Most of these serious errors have to do with English sentence form, the subject-verb pair, main clauses, and subordinate clauses. What makes a clause different from a phrase is its subject-verb pair. A main clause (or independent clause) can stand alone as a sentence, if that is what the writer wants, or it may be part of a larger sentence.

Sometimes words will be grouped together, looking like a sentence, with a capital letter at the beginning and a period at the end, but they are not actually a main clause. Something is missing; the idea is incomplete. This error is called a *fragment.*

incomplete verb	The children laughing at the monkeys.
no subject–verb pair	In the shade, three bears asleep.
no subject–verb pair	What a beautiful day!
subordinate conjunction = subordinate clause	Although signs say not to feed the animals.

The proofreader must check every sentence separately, looking for main clauses. Besides fragments, he will sometimes find *comma splices* and *fused* sentences because of main clauses inadequately joined.

comma splice	Sammy longed to see the giraffes, Brenda wanted to go directly to the sea lions.
fused	So Mom went with Sammy Dad took Brenda to the aquatic area.

The heart of the main clause, the subject–verb pair, must be in agreement; that means that both must be singular or plural. And, of course, the verb must be in the correct tense form.

verb tense error	Just yesterday we had went to the store for milk and bread.
The subject is decision, a singular noun, requiring the singular verb, was.	The decision of the parents and students were in favor of buying the computers.
The subject is dozen, plural, so the verb should be plural, are.	There is at least a dozen people in the waiting room.

Another grammatical problem that must be caught during proofreading is agreement of a different part of speech, the pronoun. Like nouns, pronouns will be either singular or plural in form. Since pronouns substitute for nouns and often follow their noun antecedents in sentences, the pronoun must match or agree with its noun antecedent.

The noun, company, is singular, so the pronoun should be singular, its.

The antecedent is one, not travelers, so the pronoun should be his.

> The company wants their employees to wear jackets at work.
>
> Only one of the travelers left their umbrella behind.

REVIEW

A proofreader must be able to recognize and correct

1. Fragments
2. Comma splices and fused sentences
3. Incorrect verb tense
4. Subject–verb disagreement
5. Pronoun–noun disagreement

OTHER ERRORS WORTH CORRECTING

Somewhat less serious mistakes that should be corrected if possible include the following.

SHIFTS

There can be confusing changes in verb tense and person (point-of-view) that simply cannot be accounted for by what is happening in the sentence. Here's an example.

The verbs shift back and forth from present tense to conditional to past without any reason.

> Every morning when I get up, I make breakfast. I would have cereal or eggs. But I like fried eggs only, not scrambled. I never ate scramble eggs.

Harcourt, Inc.

Here is an example of an inconsistency or shift in person.

> Without a plan, especially a budget, shoppers can wander around for hours and spend too much money. You have to know what your financial limits are and what you actually need. It helps to sit down a day or so ahead, look in the closet, and pay attention to the colors of your wardrobe. Otherwise, I am likely to become dizzy with all the choices and styles at my fingertips.

The subject begins as third-person shoppers, then shifts to second person you, and finally shifts again to first person I and my. The rule is to be consistent and to *avoid second person.* Formal essays are usually third person; first person is fine for personal experience, but second is too casual. Second person is appropriate for letters and instructions (as in this textbook).

UNNECESSARY COMMAS / MISSING COMMAS

It is worthwhile to memorize the five comma rules so that you do not find yourself guessing or putting commas in where you think you hear a pause (not a completely reliable guide).

Comma Rules

1. In a compound sentence, after the first main clause:

> Paul is saving his money for a car, but he hasn't chosen one yet.

2. After an introductory expression (before the main clause):

> Although it rained heavily, the crowd for the concert was huge.

3. Between items in a series:

> The nurse arrived with a thermometer, some gauze, and a syringe.

4. Around interrupting expressions:

> Those first in line, who had arrived very early, looked exhausted.

5. In dates, addresses, and to avoid misreadings:

> Ben was still living at 336 Robin Road, Atlanta, Georgia, when he
> last wrote on May 9, 1998.
> As the janitor vacuumed, the cat began to howl.

6. Never separate the subject from its verb nor the verb from its object with a comma. (This breaks the flow of the main clause.)

Not
Instead
Not
Instead

> The drill sergeant, marched the platoon daily.
> The drill sergeant marched the platoon daily.
> The news article reported, three killed.
> The news article reported three killed.

MISSING PERIODS AND QUESTION MARKS

It is remarkably easy to omit the final punctuation for a sentence. Look closely to see that a question ends in a question mark and a statement in a period.

In deciding whether to plant annuals or perennials, the gardener will ask herself two questions. Does she want the same plants, getting stronger and larger each year. Or does she want variety. If she wants a change each year, it will take time to remove and replace those annuals

Can you find the mistakes? A question mark belongs after "larger each year" and another after "variety." The last sentence ends in a period.

PROOFREADING METHODICALLY

Remember that the Creative Writer is incapable of proofreading. Put your pen down, tell him thanks very much, and send him on his way. Take a few deep breaths; get that much-needed oxygen to the brain. Bring in the Editor and use some tried-and-true methods that make proofreading effective and fast.

1. Begin at the end of the essay with the last sentence. Check it for main clauses, agreement, punctuation, then the sentence above it, and next the one above that, and so on. This method will prevent you from simply "re-reading" the essay, getting caught up in the flow of sentences, instead of actually proofreading.

2. Read out loud. This can be done, quietly, even in the classroom. Everyone else will be engrossed in his own proofing; no one will listen to you. Seldom will a serious mistake escape the ear.

3. Check only one line at a time, using a piece of paper to cover all but the line your eyes are focused on. Again, this works somewhat like reading from the bottom up; it helps the eye concentrate on one small section at a time.

WRITING SAMPLE 8

Nursing Student Reports

Some of the writing required of nursing students includes the initial assessment of a patient, a head-to-toe physical examination, charting, nurse's notes, and a variety of records such as vital signs, medications, history, and so on. These reports are generated throughout every shift and must be written on the spot. Some records are kept on flow sheets or prepared grids and involve such brief notations as date, time, amounts, check marks, abbreviations, and the like. Others require a narrative. All must be completely legible.

Here is a record called *the problem list,* taken over time from first encounter to most recent visit. Notations may be made by different nurses at different times. Notice the spelling and legibility.

No.	Date	Inactive	Chart Problem	Related to
#1	2/98	10/99	*Tachycardia 200+ bpm*	
#1A	2/98	2/98	*bp drop to 70/50 after IV digoxin*	
#1B	2/98	2/98	*Hands, face cyanotic*	
#2	**4/98**		**Chronic fatigue**	**Redefined Aug 17, 99**
#3	5/98		Diarrhea	
#4	**8/98**		**Edema, L knee, L ankle**	
#4A	**8/98**		**Joint pain, L metatarsal**	

Here is a representative entry of *narrative charting.* Again, notice the legibility. These notes are seldom in complete sentences, but in meaningful phrases that focus specifically on a procedure, a treatment, a complaint, or any facts that are important to stating problems, goals, and the progress made in relieving the patient's problems.

NURSING NOTES

Date	Time	
09/12/99	**1400**	**Deep massage provided for neck, jaw, entire back. Crackling sounds audible when fascia manipulated. States, "That hurts!"**
	1430	**Exercise demonstrated for trapezius, rhomboids, lats. Dr. T. Avery notified.**
	1445	**Complained of severe pain in L knee. Applied flourimethane.**
		R. Bowerton

WRITING SAMPLE 9

Company Newsletters

Most organizations, whether business or nonprofit, produce a newsletter to keep customers, employees, or members informed. Articles may include highlights of a regular meeting, a calendar of upcoming events, reports from the treasurer, company earnings or stock reports, interviews, recognition of accomplishments such as awards given or competitions won, and so forth. The newsletter reminds everyone involved that the organization is performing its mission.

In a perfect world, there would be few time pressures on those who write and edit newsletters. These people should have plenty of time to gather their information, draft the articles, revise, and polish everything, because the publication would appear only once a month or even quarterly. Alas, human beings being what they are, they do not send their information in to the newsletter office on time. The editor calls them, e-mails them, begs them, perhaps, or sternly insists, but somehow the writing and printing usually wind up being deadline activities.

Furthermore, it is often a relatively new employee who is assigned the newsletter responsibility, and not necessarily someone who has had any experience in this area. Therefore, writing under a time limit, once again, becomes a skill that can make the difference between success and failure.

Here is a sampling of several short articles as they might appear formatted as a company newsletter, all gathered, written, and compiled under deadline.

THE MONEY PAPER

A Financial Update from Moneymakers Investment   Spring 2000

Y2K Passes Without a Ripple

Director Main's assurances that Moneymakers Investment was completely prepared for the electronic and computer-managed changeover at the stroke of midnight at the advent of the year 2000 have proved correct.

Every account and record, all automated systems, even the lights and refrigerators in the kitchens of our offices

Around the State

Annual Meeting Slated for Whitesboro   Local officers will hear financial leader Will Fisher speak on strategies for small investors as the Dow continues to rise. Officers will consider ways to position Moneymakers to respond to overvalued technologies.

Compton Receives Honor   Agent David Compton of the Calhoun Office received the Rotary Award for Educational Excellence. Dave works with high school and college students who intern in the Moneymakers of Calhoun.

Fraud Alert!   Federal and State agencies have notified all financial institutions recently of increased contacts by scam artists who claim to be helping their "clients" benefit from Y2K changes. Their story is that if the investor wishes to avoid hidden Y2K charges at the end of the fiscal year, he should move his investment to their fund before June 30.

have come through intact, reports Kenneth Neely, Vice-President.

Thanks go to everyone who worked throughout 1999 to ensure that our facilities would be ready. And special thanks to those who stayed overnight the weekend of December 31.

On another front, we are all reminded to be vigilant for counterfeit ten, twenty, and fifty dollar bills, now that the new notes are in circulation.

CHAPTER 6

A FINAL WORD

Now you have a step-by-step approach to the timed essay. Here is another way of understanding what makes writing work. This is a non-technical way of describing your goals as a writer. In order for any piece of writing to be understood and appreciated, it must be clear, coherent, consistent, complete, and courteous.

Ways of Being *Clear*

1. Write legibly; make neat, simple corrections.
2. Choose exact words.
3. State the central idea (in a thesis statement or topic sentence).
4. Give facts and examples to support generalizations.

Ways of Being *Coherent*

1. Outline the plan of organization (the subtopics or steps).
2. Arrange the key ideas of each paragraph in an appropriate order.
3. Connect related information with transitional expressions.
4. Be logical.

Ways of Being *Consistent*

1. Stay on topic; match your answer to the question.
2. Keep the verb tense and person (pronoun case) and other grammatical forms uniform and congruent.
3. On a debatable issue, choose one side to support and stick to it.

Ways of Being *Complete*

1. Introduce the main idea *along with* the subtopics early; then repeat these key phrases in the body paragraphs.
2. Develop each paragraph fully with convincing specifics.
3. Check word endings, especially plurals and past tense.
4. Check sentences for missing words, unfinished thoughts, and missing periods.
5. Match the closing to the opening, re-emphasizing the most important idea.

Ways of Being *Courteous*

1. Assume that your reader is intelligent, interested in your ideas, but not a mind reader.

2. Assume that your subject is significant and deserves the time you are giving it, that it deserves careful presentation.

3. Make it easy for the reader to see what you have to say: allow plenty of white space.

4. Always identify yourself, your assignment, and the date.

Harcourt, Inc.

EXERCISES

MAIN CLAUSES

Exercise 1

*Mark the following sentences correct ✓ if the subject and the verb are correctly labeled, the subject with an **s** and the verb with a **v**. If either subject or verb is not correctly marked, place an **x** for incorrect.*

                            s   **v**

_____ **1.** The dead leaves blew into the swimming pool.

                            s   **v**

_____ **2.** In his hurry he forgot his lunch.

                        s **v**

_____ **3.** I talked to the professor after class.

                          v   **s**

_____ **4.** The judge sent him back to prison.

                          s   **v**

_____ **5.** A box of pencils is missing from the supplies shelf.

                        s   **v**

_____ **6.** The foul shots won the game for us.

                      s   **v**

_____ **7.** Some jumping beans were loose on the floor.

                        s   **v**

_____ **8.** Soon we had trained the parakeets to sing duets.

                      s   **v**

_____ **9.** Several of the tourists were shopping for souvenirs.

                          s   **v**

_____ **10.** Either Tom or Bill will be elected group leader.

Exercise 2

Subordinate clauses: Underline the word – the subordinating conjunction – that begins the subordinate (dependent) clause in each sentence.

1. When the crime rate rose, the city council hired more police officers.

2. I hope to go to England this summer, although I need to save more money.

3. Because of the heavy rainfall, the ball game was postponed.

4. Sue will have to skip dessert if she really wants to lose weight.

5. The librarians are searching for the book that I reserved.

6. The boys should have cleared the table before they went to the movies.

7. Even though the chapter was a long one, Jennifer worked at learning the material.

8. The door prize was won by the couple who arrived last.

9. Mother locked the door and tuned out the light after Paul came in.

10. Sara looked surprised, as if she were expecting someone else.

Exercise 3

*If the underlined words are a __main clause__, put a ✓ on the blank; if not, put an **x**.*

_____ 1. Having lived in Britain for years, Bill Bryson knew all about British idiosyncrasies.

_____ 2. One such notion is that Britain is a big place.

_____ 3. Because most Americans would drive thirty miles for a taco, it seems peculiar to think that a trip from London to Cornwall is too long for one day.

_____ 4. The southwest coast of England is between 200 and 250 miles from central London, depending on how far you care to go.

_____ 5. Still, there are some Britishers who will say you should have left yesterday.

_____ 6. Bryson believes that the British have a totally private sense of distance; they pretend that Britain is a lonely island in the middle of an empty sea.

_____ 7. Bryson worked in England as a newspaper writer; and he married an English girl.

_____ 8. Not long ago, the Brysons decided to move to America.

_____ 9. Before he left, Bill wanted to revisit as many places in England and Scotland as he could.

_____ **10.** <u>Because he loved the country so</u>, despite British idiosyncrasies, he decided to travel around the country before he left for America.

_____ **11.** He wrote a book about <u>his travels called *Notes From a Small Island*.</u>

_____ **12.** Once when younger he failed to find a hotel in Dover, so <u>he slept on the ground with his backpack for a pillow.</u>

_____ **13.** It grew cold in the night, so he pulled clothes out of his backpack and put them all on, <u>including a pair of boxer shorts for his head.</u>

_____ **14.** Early the next morning <u>he began searching for someplace to have breakfast.</u>

_____ **15.** <u>He met an old guy walking a dog</u> who said, "Might turn out nice."

_____ **16.** The man directed him to a transport cafe (<u>a cafe for truck drivers</u>) and suggested "You might want to take them pants off your head before you go in."

_____ **17.** <u>When Bryson did finally locate a room</u>, it was in the boarding-house of one Mrs. Gubbins.

_____ **18.** <u>Mrs. Gubbins explained the house rules</u>, one of which was that guests must vacate the premises during the middle of the day.

_____ **19.** She also showed him how to flush the loo, where to wipe his feet on entry, and <u>how to operate the heater in the bedroom.</u>

_____ **20.** Bryson felt that it was hard to tell <u>which was worse</u>, spending the night on the ground or staying at Mrs. Gubbins' boarding-house.

FRAGMENTS

Exercise 4

In the following paired items, one is a complete sentence, one is a fragment. Place an **x** *in front of the fragment.*

1. _____ **a.** Blows his horn and tailgates cars.

_____ **b.** The aggressive driver blows his horn and tailgates cars.

2. _____ **a.** By speeding could cause a serious accident.

_____ **b.** By speeding the careless driver could cause a serious accident.

3. _____ **a.** School uniforms save money and discourage class competition.

_____ **b.** Although school uniforms save money and discourage class competition.

4. ____ **a.** We should have seen it coming.
   ____ **b.** Because we should have seen it coming.
5. ____ **a.** When everything is said and done.
   ____ **b.** When everything is said and done, the work was good for me.
6. ____ **a.** For example, gasoline may cost as little as $0.95 a gallon.
   ____ **b.** For example: gasoline, oil changes, maintenance repairs.
7. ____ **a.** The worst consequence of all, for the sheltered adolescent.
   ____ **b.** Imprisonment is the worst consequence of all.
8. ____ **a.** Under the car and behind the garage.
   ____ **b.** We looked under the car and behind the garage.
9. ____ **a.** Everyone to contribute to the office coffee fund.
   ____ **b.** Everyone was asked to contribute to the office coffee fund.
10. ____ **a.** No one expected the violent thunderstorms.
    ____ **b.** Even if no one expected the violent thunderstorms.
11. ____ **a.** Once upon a time, a king had two sons.
    ____ **b.** Once upon a time.
12. ____ **a.** Not only is working full-time sure to tire the student.
    ____ **b.** Not only is working full-time sure to tire the student, it will seriously interfere with his study time.

COMMA SPLICE AND FUSED SENTENCES

Exercise 5

*First, underline the subjects once and the predicates twice. Next, decide whether the comma is "splicing" together two **main clauses** or simply following an introductory expression or working with a coordinating conjunction in a compound sentence. In the blank in front of each item, write **cs** for comma splice or a ✓ for correct. If there is no punctuation of any kind between two main clauses, mark the item **F** for fused.*

____ **1.** The restaurant parking lot was full, we drove around waiting for someone to pull out.

____ **2.** After a few minutes, we found a place for the car and went inside.

____ **3.** The crowd was pressed together in a long line, and an attendant was taking names.

____ **4.** We were told the wait would be less than ten minutes that would be acceptable.

____ **5.** However, it was more than twenty minutes later when we were seated.

____ **6.** Now we were really hungry, we read our menus eagerly.

____ **7.** We looked around for waiters, frustration mounted.

____ **8.** Suddenly, a young man in a big white apron appeared and poured our water.

Harcourt, Inc.

_____   **9.** "We're ready to order," we said, "I'll find you a waiter," he said, we never saw him again.

_____   **10.** Naturally, the crowd was slowing down things in the kitchen.

_____   **11.** We couldn't blame the help because it was a busy night, but we considered leaving.

_____   **12.** Andy suggested that we play a game to take our minds off our stomachs, everyone agreed.

_____   **13.** It seemed like no time at all, our waiter appeared and apologized for our delay.

_____   **14.** In just minutes, we all had salads and were digging in.

_____   **15.** It was actually one of the best evenings I can remember, the food was great, we soon forgot all about the slow start.

Exercise 6

If the item is a correctly punctuated sentence, mark a ✓ ; if it is a comma splice or fused sentence, mark **x**.

_____   **1.** London has a long history, in 55 BC Julius Caesar's troops found a few tribesmen living on the banks of the Thames River there.

_____   **2.** When the Roman troops returned in 33 AD, a small port and trading community had been established.

_____   **3.** The Romans invaded and set up headquarters on the north bank, they called the place Londinium.

_____   **4.** Over the years London grew steadily, and when the Normans (French) conquered the Saxons in 1066, it was made the national capital.

_____   **5.** The original city was surrounded by a wall, remnants of the old wall can be visited by tourists today.

_____   **6.** Almost all of the old city was destroyed by the Great Fire of 1666, so the buildings of central London today date from the seventeenth century.

_____   **7.** Soon London grew up to and enveloped nearby settlements like Westminster, the growth was explosive and made London the biggest and wealthiest city in the world.

_____   **8.** Unfortunately, the hopes of wealth attracted many unemployed who crowded into the eastern dock area, this area soon became an unsanitary slum.

_____   **9.** By the late 1800s, 4.5 million people lived in inner London, with another 4 million nearby.

_____ **10.** In World War II, German bombing devastated the center of the city, necessitating another rebuilding effort, during this period many of the docks disappeared.

_____ **11.** Today a visitor to the Museum of London can see sections of the old Roman wall and a beautiful second century mosaic, there is also sculpture from the Temple of Mithras.

_____ **12.** Mithras was a Roman deity that protected the good from evil, the temple came to light when a World War II bomb plowed into the site.

_____ **13.** There is no exact date for the end of the Ancient Period and the beginning of the Medieval London, but by the eleventh century the king, Edward the Confessor, established his court and abbey at Westminster.

_____ **14.** Also during the eleventh century, city tradesmen established guilds, protective organizations similar to modern trade unions, these groups were very powerful.

_____ **15.** Disease was rife in the crowded, unsanitary city, probably overcrowding kept the population to no more than 50,000 during this time.

_____ **16.** Another medieval institution was the Tower of London, where political prisoners could be taken for almost any reason.

_____ **17.** The most famous English writer of the medieval period is Geoffrey Chaucer, his _Canterbury Tales_ are still read all over the world for their engaging pictures of fourteenth century England.

_____ **18.** One of London's best-known structures dates from the medieval period, London Bridge, the first stone bridge, built in 1209.

_____ **19.** The next stage of London history is called the Elizabethan period, it was during the reign of Elizabeth I that England became a world sea power.

_____ **20.** The Elizabethan period is also widely known for the work of the playwright Shakespeare, whose Globe Theater on the south bank of the Thames has recently been restored.

SINGULAR AND PLURAL FORMS

Exercise 7

Circle the letter of the correct answer. (The dictionary can help you identify parts of speech and plural forms.)

1. Which nouns are <u>plural</u>?
   a. news, scientist   **b.** chooses, eats   **c.** children, mice

2. Which pronouns are <u>singular</u>?
   a. their, ours   **b.** everybody, no one   **c.** themselves, those

3. Which verbs are <u>singular</u>?
   a. tastes, votes   **b.** eat, investigate   **c.** have seen, are racing

4. Choose the <u>verb</u> that agrees with its subjects.
   Either Washington or Adams (**a.** wants   **b.** want) the trip postponed.

5. Choose the <u>subject</u> that agrees with the verb.
   There comes to my mind the (**a.** answer   **b.** answers) to the question.

6. Choose the <u>verb</u> that matches the subject.
   Why (**a.** is   **b.** are) an alarm system and a guard dog both necessary?

7. Choose the <u>subject</u> that matches the verb.
   (**a.** A number   **b.** The number) of visitors to the park increases every year.

8. Choose the <u>pronoun</u> that matches its antecedent.
   A large company usually provides (**a.** its   **b.** their) employees free parking.

9. Choose the <u>verb</u> that matches its subject (and antecedent).
   Eliot is one of those poets who (**a.** makes   **b.** make) symbols memorable.

10. Choose the <u>pronoun</u> that matches its antecedent.
   Anybody in the first line may have (**a.** his   **b.** their) choice of a cap or a pen.

AGREEMENT

Exercise 8

Underline the <u>verb</u> that matches the subject.

1. Evil and suffering (has, have) always troubled mankind.

2. Myths, in part, (is, are) attempts to explain the existence of evil.

3. The Pandora myth (offers, offer) one such explanation.

4. According to one version, men (was, were) on earth long before women.

5. Then the chief of the gods (becomes, become) angry when another god (cares, care) too much for these mortals.

6. He (decides, decide) to take revenge on men by creating something irresistible but evil.

Harcourt, Inc.

7. And so Zeus (creates, create) woman.

8. She (was, were) called Pandora – "the gift of all" – because all the gods sent gifts to make her beautiful.

9. According to this version, women (is, are) the source of all evil.

10. Although this story is unpopular today, it (is, are) not very different from most versions of Eve's persuading Adam to eat the forbidden apple.

Exercise 9

Underline the <u>subject</u> that matches the verb.

1. (Pandora), in other (versions), is not evil, merely curious.

2. (All) of the (gods) put an evil in a box and seal it.

3. (They) give the (box) to Pandora, but tell her never to open it.

4. The (gods) then send (her) to Epimetheus to be his wife.

5. (Epimetheus), whose (name) means "afterthought," is not very bright.

6. His (brother) Prometheus ("forethought") has told him never to accept a gift from Zeus.

7. Still, (everything, they) goes well for awhile.

8. But then (Pandora's) (curiosity) gets the better of her; she has to see what's in that box.

9. When (she) opens (it), all the evils and sorrows swarm out.

10. She rushes to slam the (lid) , but only one (thing) is left in the box – hope.

VERB FORMS

Exercise 10

Underline the correct verb tense.

1. In my last high school class I (wrote, had wrote) only one essay.

2. Since the beginning of this semester I (have wrote, have written) three essays.

3. Jim hasn't (saw, seen) his tutor yet.

4. Nicole (has went, has gone) to her computer class.

5. The Internet (has become, has became) a vital source of information of all kinds.

6. When we (saw, seen) how easy it is, we asked our parents to get on the net.

7. Sara prefers ballet to the Internet; she (begin, began) lessons this year.

8. No one could have (knowed, known) she would learn so fast.

9. Sara met Abby at ballet, and they (growed, grew) to be great friends.

10. When I saw the mess in the kitchen, I thought the dog (did, done) it.

11. Naturally, after Boomer (ate, had ate) the brownies, he was sick.

12. None of us had (saw, seen) the puppy Dave bought.

13. He (choosed, chose) a golden retriever.

14. I have a friend who (thinks, would think) that snakes make the best pets.

15. How many sandwiches have you (took, taken)?

16. Jason thought he would be blamed when the window was (broke, broken).

17. Everyone was tired after volleyball and decided to (lie, lay) on the grass.

18. It took two hours to have a key made when I (lost, losed) mine.

19. The car has been (drove, driven) in mud and not washed.

20. It has been a year since I (flew, flown) anywhere.

SHIFTS

Exercise 11

Underline any pronouns in first or second person and replace them with a third-person substitute.

1. Some dieters seem to believe that you can live on grapefruit and lose seven or more pounds a week.

2. They don't think this is dangerous for you.

3. Others prefer to cut back on the sugar and carbohydrates you eat.

4. Dieting is big business, and it is no surprise that you see so many pitches on television for magic pills to make you lose weight.

5. Diseases like bulimia and anorexia can kill you.

6. Even prescribed medicines like Fen-Phen can give you serious physical problems that you cannot heal easily.

7. If you think some diet plan sounds too good to be true, it probably is.

Harcourt, Inc.

8. You need discipline to count calories and say no to desserts.

9. Everyone knows that daily exercise is important, but you have to be committed to that, too.

10. If you are trying to look like a Barbie doll, that could be your first mistake.

Exercise 12

Correct verb tense shifts in these sentences.

1. The work itself is not difficult, but it is the frustrations that made me unhappy.

2. As I moved the boxes to the table, the boss's little son comes in and knocks them onto the floor.

3. I thought it over and decide to look for another job.

4. After all, if I am frustrated all day, I wouldn't come home satisfied.

5. Even though I like my employer, who was a friendly man, I can probably find work that suits me better.

6. I am looking for work in food service and wanted to get experience as a cook.

7. It is important to work for someone respected in his field and do not expect a high salary at first.

8. Actually, good cooks do make good money, but the creativity was probably more important to them.

9. As soon as I walk into a kitchen, I felt better.

10. My mind began coming up with a dozen ideas for the meal I am about to prepare.

COMMA RULES

Exercise 13

Missing Commas: The following sentences should have commas, but do not. Mark the sentence <u>a</u> if it is a compound sentence, <u>b</u> if an introductory expression precedes the main clause, <u>c</u> if there are items in a series, <u>d</u> if there is an interrupting expression, or <u>e</u> if there is a date, address, or misreading can occur.

_____   **1.** I want to learn to use the Internet but the computers in the library seem to be always occupied.

_____   **2.** When I have a break between classes the computer lab has a class in it.

_____ **3.** There should be computers in the Student Center in the halls and in the dining hall if necessary.

_____ **4.** I have to come back to the library at night which is seriously inconvenient to get my assignment done.

_____ **5.** We are told that by February 1 2001 ten new computers will be installed.

_____ **6.** By then however I will have finished this literature course.

_____ **7.** My professor wants us to find something called The Electronic Beowulf Project and I would if I could just get on-line.

_____ **8.** Although my dad likes everything electronic he hasn't put our home computer on-line yet.

_____ **9.** Perhaps he needs a modem more ram or a bargain price.

_____ **10.** I've got to find a way to motivate him or I'll be spending every evening in the library.

_____ **11.** My friend Mark who is also in my literature class uses the Internet to shop for used cars.

_____ **12.** Naturally he does that only after finishing his homework.

_____ **13.** Even my little brother surfs the net and he's only ten.

_____ **14.** He's been taking a computer class since August and knows how to run a search refine a search and bookmark locations.

_____ **15.** No matter what I am going to become an Internet player.

Exercise 14

Correct Commas: Mark the sentence <u>a</u> if it is compound, <u>b</u> if it begins with an introductory expression, <u>c</u> if commas separate items in a series, <u>d</u> if an interrupter is marked off from the main clause, or <u>e</u> if there is an address, date, or misreading would occur.

_____ **1.** My dad's doctor told him he needed to relax, but he didn't say how.

_____ **2.** After all, it's not easy for a fifty-year-old who has been working hard for years to suddenly "relax."

_____ **3.** Should he take up golf, fishing, bungee jumping?

_____ **4.** I was just kidding about bungee jumping, but my dad hasn't a clue.

_____ **5.** If he hangs around the house, he gets on my mom's nerves.

_____ **6.** She suggested that he take up gardening, but all his flowers died.

_____ **7.** Worse than that, he somehow killed the grass too.

_____ **8.** Mom threatened to do something he'd regret, so I took him with me to shoot a few hoops.

_____ **9.** Soon we were circling each other, faking rushes, shooting from impossible distances.

_____ **10.** We weren't making many shots, but we were laughing uproariously.

_____ **11.** I was just congratulating myself on getting my dad relaxed when, without warning, he fell flat.

_____ **12.** Believe it or not, he stepped on his shoelace.

_____ **13.** He was out cold, and I was scared to death.

_____ **14.** I drove him to the emergency room, called his doctor, and filled out forms.

_____ **15.** Later his doctor told me that if he'd known Dad would have such trouble relaxing, he would have given him a hypo to begin with.

DICTION

Exercise 15

Replace the vague wording with more exact and meaningful phrasing. Underline the best replacement.

1. Isn't this a <u>nice</u> day?
  a. delicious   **b.** cooperative   **c.** beautiful

2. Mr. Clayton is the <u>nicest</u> boss I've ever worked for.
  a. delicious   **b.** most cooperative   **c.** beautiful

3. A <u>nice</u> meal is one of my favorite treats to myself.
  a. delicious   **b.** cooperative   **c.** beautiful

4. This oceanside town is expecting <u>a lot of</u> tourists in June.
  a. some   **b.** thousands   **c.** numbers of

5. <u>A lot of</u> noise makes studying difficult.
  a. Deafening   **b.** Tons of   **c.** Too much

6. Please give me <u>a lot of</u> gravy!
  a. plenty of   **b.** two helpings of   **c.** more

7. All these <u>people</u> want to see their team win.
   a. fans   **b.** students   **c.** readers

8. When <u>people</u> stay within the speed limit, the roads are safer for every-one.
   a. citizens   **b.** drivers   **c.** voters

9. The doctor's waiting room was filled with <u>people</u>, some of whom had been waiting an hour or more.
   a. children   **b.** nurses   **c.** patients

10. Mondays were <u>a big day</u> for Ed, starting at 7:00 a.m. and not ending until dark.
    a. important   **b.** long   **c.** delightful

Exercise 16

Replace the cliches with more exact, literal wording. Underline the best replacement.

1. They resent the new captain because he's a <u>hot dog</u>.
   a. cheap   **b.** showoff   **c.** underqualified

2. I'm afraid my computer is <u>a lemon</u>.
   a. faulty   **b.** too expensive   **c.** complicated to operate

3. Relax, <u>it's all downhill from here</u>.
   a. it's doomed to failure   **b.** it's a short distance
   c. it's easier from here on

4. Her face is <u>an open book</u>.
   a. stiff   **b.** a reflection of her feelings   **c.** blank

5. The math exam is <u>a piece of cake</u>.
   a. very easy   **b.** misleading   **c.** sweet

6. These figures are <u>in the ballpark</u>.
   a. a waste of time   **b.** within expectations   **c.** frivolous

7. I'm not going to <u>open that can of worms</u>.
   a. create complications   **b.** raise questions   **c.** seem ignorant

8. We don't want to <u>throw the baby out with the bath water</u>.
   a. be monsters   **b.** make a mistake
   c. confuse the trivial with the vital

9. My grandfather is always <u>there for me</u>.
   a. at home   **b.** a good example   **c.** ready to support me

10. This tax question is <u>a hot potato.</u>
    a. unhealthy   **b.** a sensitive, risky issue   **c.** illegal

MORE PRACTICE ESSAY TOPICS

Remember, the wording of a topic will often indicate a fitting method of organizing the discussion. Of course, when no particular clues appear in the question, several methods can be combined to develop a convincing essay. Tactics always effective are exemplification, description, and definition.

1. When teenagers begin dating, they usually take great pains to make a good impression on their date's parents. However, sometimes they make mistakes. What are the worst things a young man or woman might do to make a bad impression on the parents of his or her date?

2. Explain the difference between the terms "love" and "infatuation." Be specific.

3. How do you explain the great popularity of yard sales? Go into some detail.

4. If you had to choose to spend an afternoon at a stock car race or a museum, which would you prefer? Explain your choice.

5. Everybody eats, but does one person get stuck doing all the cooking? Agree or disagree that one of the life skills everyone over the age of fifteen should have is being able to cook a basic meal or two.

6. If you were the boss, for what reasons would you fire an employee? Explain.

7. Should politicians be able to expect to live their lives with some degree of privacy? How much?

8. While it is easy to criticize politicians for their shortcomings, it would be going too far to say that they are all a bunch of crooks. Name an elected official you consider ideal or nearly ideal and explain what makes him or her a model politician.

9. When college students are considering what major to choose, what is more important to them, in your opinion, their eventual earning power or making a contribution to society? Discuss with examples.

CHAPTER 8

ANSWER KEY

CHAPTER 2
Review Questions
1. b
2. b
3. c
4. c

5. a
6. d
7. c
8. d

CHAPTER 3
Exercise 1
1. boxes
2. children
3. cities
4. freshmen
5. heroes

6. leaves
7. mice
8. skies
9. teeth
10. wages

Exercise 2
1. create, creation, creative
2. decide, decision, decisive
3. engage, engagement, engaging
4. harmonize, harmony, harmonious
5. hate, hatred, hateful
6. infuriate, fury, furious
7. immunize, immunity, immune
8. indicate, indication, indicative
9. laugh, laughter, laughable
10. negate, negation, negative
11. obey, obedience, obedient
12. prefer, preference, preferable
13. resolve, resolution, resolute
14. terrify, terror, terrible, -fied
15. weigh, weight, weighty

CHAPTER 7
Exercise 1
✓ 1.
x 2.

✓ 3.
x 4.

x 5.
x 6.
x 7.

✓ 8.
✓ 9.
x 10.

Exercise 2
1. When
2. although
3. Because
4. if
5. that
6. before

7. Even though
8. who
9. after
10. as if

Exercise 3
x 1.
x 2.
✓ 3.
x 4.
x 5.
✓ 6.
✓ 7.
x 8.
x 9.
x 10.

x 11.
✓ 12.
x 13.
✓ 14.
✓ 15.
x 16.
x 17.
✓ 18.
x 19.
x 20.

Exercise 4
1. a
2. a
3. b
4. b
5. a
6. b

7. a
8. a
9. a
10. b
11. b
12. a

Exercise 5
cs 1. lot was; we drove
✓ 2. we found and went
✓ 3. crowd was pressed; attendant was taking

F **4.** We were told; that would be

✓ **5.** it was; we were seated

CS **6.** we were; we read

CS **7.** we looked; frustration mounted

✓ **8.** man appeared and poured

CS **9.** We're; we said; I'll find; he said; we saw

✓ **10.** crowd was slowing

✓ **11.** we could blame; it was; we considered

CS **12.** Andy suggested; we play; everyone agreed

CS **13.** It seemed; waiter appeared and apologized

✓ **14.** we had and were digging in

CS **15.** It was; I can remember; food was; we forgot

Exercise 6

X	**1.**	**X**	**11.**
✓	**2.**	**X**	**12.**
X	**3.**	✓	**13.**
✓	**4.**	**X**	**14.**
X	**5.**	**X**	**15.**
✓	**6.**	✓	**16.**
X	**7.**	**X**	**17.**
X	**8.**	**X**	**18.**
✓	**9.**	**X**	**19.**
X	**10.**	✓	**20.**

Exercise 7

1. c		**6.** b
2. b		**7.** b
3. a		**8.** a
4. a		**9.** b
5. a		**10.** a

Exercise 8

1. have		**6.** decides
2. are		**7.** creates
3. offers		**8.** was
4. were		**9.** are
5. becomes, cares		**10.** is

Exercise 9

1. Pandora		**3.** They
2. All		**4.** gods

5. Epimetheus **8.** curiosity
6. brother **9.** she
7. everything **10.** thing

Exercise 10

1. wrote		**11.** ate
2. have written		**12.** seen
3. see		**13.** chose
4. has gone		**14.** thinks
5. has become		**15.** taken
6. saw, asked		**16.** broken
7. began		**17.** lie
8. known		**18.** lost
9. grew		**19.** driven
10. did		**20.** flew

Exercise 11

1. <u>you</u>; they
2. <u>you</u>; them
3. <u>you</u>; they
4. <u>you</u> see; there are
5. <u>you</u>; can kill (no pronoun)
6. give <u>you</u>; can produce
7. <u>you</u>; If some diet (no pronoun)
8. <u>You</u> need; It takes
9. <u>you</u> have to be committed; that takes commitment, too.
10. <u>you</u>; <u>your</u>; Trying to look like a Barbie doll could be a mistake.

Exercise 12

1. make		**7.** not to expect
2. came, knocked		
3. decided		**8.** is
4. will not		**9.** feel
5. is		**10.** begins
6. want		

Exercise 13

1. a		**9.** c
2. b		**10.** a
3. c		**11.** d
4. d		**12.** b
5. e		**13.** a
6. d		**14.** c
7. a		**15.** b
8. b		

Exercise 14

1. a		**3.** c
2. b		**4.** a

5. b	**11.** d	**5.** a	**8.** b
6. a	**12.** b	**6.** b	**9.** c
7. b	**13.** a	**7.** a	**10.** b
8. a	**14.** c		
9. c	**15.** b	**Exercise 16**	
10. a		**1.** b	**6.** b
		2. a	**7.** a
Exercise 15		**3.** c	**8.** c
1. c	**3.** a	**4.** b	**9.** c
2. b	**4.** b	**5.** a	**10.** b

INDEX

Harcourt, Inc.